Lecture Notes in Computer Science 4606

Commenced Publication in 1973
Founding and Former Series Editors:
Gerhard Goos, Juris Hartmanis, and Jan van Leeuwen

Editorial Board

Aiko Pras   Marten van Sinderen (Eds.)

Dependable and Adaptable Networks and Services

13th Open European Summer School and
IFIP TC6.6 Workshop, EUNICE 2007
Enschede, The Netherlands, July 18-20, 2007
Proceedings

 Springer

Volume Editors

Aiko Pras
Marten van Sinderen
University of Twente
Faculty of EEMCS
PO Box 217, 7500 AE, Enschede, The Netherlands
E-mail: {A.Pras,M.J.vanSinderen}@ewi.utwente.nl

Library of Congress Control Number: 2007930222

CR Subject Classification (1998): C.2, C.3, D.4, D.2, H.4, H.3, H.5, K.4

LNCS Sublibrary: SL 3 – Information Systems and Application, incl. Internet/
Web and HCI

ISSN   0302-9743
ISBN-10   3-540-73529-1 Springer Berlin Heidelberg New York
ISBN-13   978-3-540-73529-8 Springer Berlin Heidelberg New York

Springer is a part of Springer Science+Business Media

springer.com

© Springer-Verlag Berlin Heidelberg 2007
Printed in Germany

Typesetting: Camera-ready by author, data conversion by Scientific Publishing Services, Chennai, India
Printed on acid-free paper   SPIN: 12088300   06/3180   5 4 3 2 1 0

Preface

The main goal of the EUNICE Summer School is to give young researchers, and particularly PhD students, the opportunity to present their work at an international level. The EUNICE Summer School also seeks to offer comprehensive and inspiring invited talks from experienced experts in the field, providing a context for discussions on ongoing research and new challenges.

The EUNICE Summer School is an initiative of the European University Network of Information and Communication Engineering, or EUNICE Network for short. Although the summer school events are organized by the member institutions taking turns, submission to and participation in the events are open to researchers outside the EUNICE Network.

The 13th EUNICE Summer School returned to Enschede, The Netherlands, where it was hosted earlier in 2000. Back in 2000, the theme of the summer school was 'Innovative Internet Applications.' Much has changed since then: wireless network technologies have become a constantly growing part of the Internet infrastructure, and increasingly smaller and more powerful computing devices with flexible connectivity open the possibility of new services and applications.

The EUNICE 2007 theme, 'Dependable and Adaptable Networks and Services,' linked to this change and how it affects and is affected by research in the field of information and communication technology. One of the main challenges in the next decade will be to make the Internet and the services that are provided on top of it more dependable and adaptable. Research on this theme is needed for fixed, wireless and ad-hoc networking, ubiquitous communication and computing, sensor networks, and context-awareness. While individual mobile applications with context-aware and personalized features emerged, at the same time many challenges for network and service architectures were imposed concerning integration, interoperability, management, provisioning, reliability and security. On the one hand research has to make available a sound understanding of these applications and their supporting service and network architectures. On the other hand, research should produce service and network infrastructure solutions to be able to provide the necessary quality of service for the envisioned applications.

We received many submissions on these topics, but unfortunately could only accept 17 papers for presentation at the summer school. A fair evaluation and selection of papers was only possible thanks to the first-class reviews, at least three per submitted paper, from our Program Committee members. The accepted papers were grouped as follows in sessions for the single-track technical program: (1) Middleware and Supportive Services, (2) Context-Awareness, (3) Voice over IP, (4) User Behavior, Security and Legal Aspects, (5) Performance Aspects, and (6) Novel Architectures. This technical program was complemented with four invited keynotes.

We would like to take this opportunity to express our thanks and gratitude to the sponsors and supporters of the 13th EUNICE Summer School: IFIP TC6 Working Group 6.6, IEEE Communications Society, Euro-NGI, EMANICS, Springer, NWO, and CTIT.

Many people worked very hard to make this summer school a success. Special thanks go tothe Program Committee members for their efforts necessary to maintain the high-quality standard of the EUNICE Summer School, to Annelies Klos for her essential support in to the local organization, and to Remco van de Meent for his contribution during the preparation of the conference proceedings.

May 2007

Aiko Pras
Marten van Sinderen

EUNICE — Member Charter

European Network of Universities and Companies in Information and Communication Engineering.

1 Mission

The European universities and companies signing this charter are anxious to improve in a permanent manner the quality and relevance of their teaching and research in the field of information and communication technologies. They declare their desire to co-operate in the following ways:

- By jointly developing and promoting the best and compatible standard of European higher education and professionals in information and communication technologies
- By increasing scientific and technical knowledge in the field of telecommunications and developing their applications in the economy

2 Membership

The network is made up of European universities within the European Union and outside it, whether from Western, Central or Eastern Europe. These universities are involved at their own appropriate organization level, taking into account the mission of the network. The parties signing the present charter will be the "founding partners." Other universities, very limited in number, might be invited to join the network as "members."

Transnational companies, working together with the universities on information and communication technologies, and representatives from the relevant commission of the European Union will be offered the opportunity to be associate members. No institution can apply for membership.

3 Education

The partners will seek the development of high-level compatibility of the existing or commonly developed courses and programs, in order to facilitate their recognition by employers independently of their geographical location in Europe. To achieve this goal, the partners will, inside the network, work on mutual recognition of these courses and programs.

To develop interculturality, these courses and programs will be accessible in such a way as to encourage, as far as possible, long-duration mobility for students and faculty members from one country to another (i.e., several months). To set compatible standards, shorter-duration operations will be conducted such as:

- Summer schools for young faculty members and PhD students
- Intensive seminars, in limited numbers, for students
- Short-duration mobility for faculty members for teaching assignments
- Use of new technologies in education

Finally, the partners will take advantage of the network of relations set up as described above to develop common modules for onsite training, for the world industry.

4 Research

The partners will also take advantage of this network to collaborate on research and development projects which could be carried out in common by several of them and which could lead to marketable applications in particular.

5 Organization and Structure

To achieve the above-mentioned aims, the institutions concerned will form a flexible structure whose role will be to think about and decide on joint actions. It will be called the steering group and will meet twice a year. The network would have no legal status. However, the network may authorize a member or set of members to act on its behalf.

Concrete proposition in education and research will be worked out in small working groups of at least two partners, chosen by the steering group as opportunities arise. Finally, a permanent secretariat, located at France Telecom University, will be established to co-ordinate all the information relevant to the network's activities.

6 Means and Finance

The institutions concerned will provide the specific financial and/or inkind support necessary for the smooth running of the network, notably human resources (research lecturers, engineers, administrators, etc.).

The partners in the network will share information about funding opportunities and seek, as often as necessary, financial aid from public authorities for its actions:

- Within each country
- From bilateral programs at a country level, whenever such financial aids exist
- And finally at the European level by means of community schemes (ERASMUS, COMETT, TEMPUS, RACE, ESPRIT,..., scientific and technological co-operation with Central and Eastern Europe, ..., human resources and mobility, etc.)

All things being equal regarding a specific action within the scope of the network, a member will prefer co-operation with other members of the network.

EUNICE Member Institutions

Finland	Tampere University of Technology
France	ENST Bretagne, Brest
	ENST Paris
	Loria University Poincaré, Nancy
	Telecom INT, Evry
Germany	Universität Karlsruhe
	Technische Universität München
	Universität Stuttgart
Hungary	Budapest University of Technology and Economics
Italy	Politecnico di Torino
Netherlands	University of Twente
Norway	Norwegian University of Science and Technology, Trondheim
Russia	St. Petersburg State University of Telecommunications
Spain	Universidad Carlos III de Madrid
	Universitat Politècnica de Catalunya
	Technical University of Madrid
UK	University of Sussex
	University College London

Organization

EUNICE 2007 was organised by the Centre for Telematics and Information Technology of the University of Twente, The Netherlands.

Technical Program Committee Co-chairs

Aiko Pras   University of Twente, The Netherlands
Marten van Sinderen   University of Twente, The Netherlands

Local Organization

Aiko Pras   University of Twente, The Netherlands
Annelies Klos   University of Twente, The Netherlands
Marten van Sinderen   University of Twente, The Netherlands

EUNICE 2007 Technical Program Committee

Arturo Azcorra	Carlos III University, Spain
Boudewijn Haverkort	University of Twente, The Netherlands
Burkhard Stiller	University of Zürich and ETH Zürich, Switzerland
Carlos Delgado Kloos	Carlos III University, Spain
Daniel Kofman	ENST Paris, France
David Larrabeiti	Carlos III University, Spain
Edit Halász	Budapest University of Technology and Economics, Hungary
Finn Aagesen	NTNU, Norway
Hermann De Meer	University of Passau, Germany
Isabelle Chrisment	Henri Poincaré University, France
Jarmo Harju	Tampere University of Technology, Finland
Joerg Eberspaecher	Technical University of Munich, Germany
Juergen Schoenwaelder	Jacobs University Bremen, Germany
Luís Ferreira Pires	University of Twente, The Netherlands
Mark Burgess	University College Oslo, Norway
Markus Fiedler	BTH, Sweden
Martin Köhn	University of Freiburg, Germany
Maryline Laurent-Maknavicius	Laurent-Maknavicius, INT, France
Matthias Hollick	TU Darmstadt, Germany
Maurice Gagnaire	ENST, France
Maurizio Munafò	Turin Polytechnic, Italy
Mikhail Smirnov	Fraunhofer FOKUS, Germany
Olivier Festor	LORIA-INRIA, France

Paul Kühn	University of Stuttgart, Germany
Ralf Lehnert	TU Dresden, Germany
Ralf Steinmetz	TU Darmstadt, Germany
Robert Szabo	Budapest University of Technology and Economics, Hungary
Rolv Braek	Norwegian University of Science and Technology, Norway
Samir Tohmé	Versailles Saint-Quentin-en-Yvelines University, France
Sebastian Abeck	University of Karlsruhe, Germany
Sebastian Sallent	TU Catalunya, Spain
Tamas Henk	Budapest University of Technology and Economics, Hungary
Thomas Plagemann	University of Oslo, Norway
Tibor Cinkler	Budapest University of Technology and Economics, Hungary
Yvon Kermarrec	ENST Bretagne, France

Sponsors

Centre for Telematics and Information Technology
EMANICS Network of Excellence
Euro-NGI Network of Excellence
IEEE Communications Society
IFIP TC6 Working Group 6.6
Nederlandse Organisatie voor Wetenschappelijk Onderzoek
Springer

Table of Contents

Technical Session 4: User Behavior, Security and Legal Aspects

Technical Session 5: Performance Aspects

Technical Session 6: Novel Architectures

Identity as a Service –
Towards a Service-Oriented
Identity Management Architecture

Christian Emig, Frank Brandt, Sebastian Kreuzer, and Sebastian Abeck

Cooperation & Management, Universität Karlsruhe (TH), 76128 Karlsruhe
{emig, brandt, kreuzer, abeck}@cm-tm.uka.de

Abstract. Service-oriented architecture (SOA) will form the basis of future information systems. Web services are a promising way to implement SOA enabling the loose coupling of functionality at service interfaces. The focus in SOA changes from traditional software systems to reusable, business-relevant services. Considering the cross-cutting concern of identity management (IdM), it is still an open issue how to construct an SOA-aware IdM architecture enabling "identity as a service" and how to loosely couple the IdM services with SOA's core concern part. In this paper we present a blueprint for a service-oriented identity management architecture featuring interoperability by applying existing standards. Our solution has been tested and evaluated in an implementation case study.

1 Introduction

1.1 Background on Web Service-Oriented Architecture

Currently most enterprises try to align their business processes with the supporting IT by migrating to service-oriented architecture (SOA). Web service technologies are commonly recognized as a promising way for the implementation of SOA; in the following, we focus on web service-oriented architectures (WSOA). With the mutual consent to use WSDL (Web Services Description Language, [1]) for the definition of service interfaces and SOAP (Simple Object Access Protocol, [2]) as the communication protocol, the cornerstone for interoperability is set. Bottom-up approaches start with existing applications and wrap their business functionality to web services. Integration can then be done by composing web services of heterogeneous software systems using process execution languages like BPEL (Business Process Execution Language). Top-down approaches focus business processes and their mapping to composite and basic web services. This allows business analysts to perform "programming-in-the-large", the system-independent orchestration of business-related (web) services along business processes [3].

1.2 Motivation for Identity Management in Web Service-Oriented Architecture

Besides the development of WSOA's core concern part there are several cross-cutting concerns that have to be addressed: a central one is to enable security, especially

A. Pras and M. van Sinderen (Eds.): EUNICE 2007, LNCS 4606, pp. 1–8, 2007.

access control. Access control consists of authentication and authorization verification. Looking at the mass and complexity of the existing and upcoming standards in the web service security area like WS-Security, SAML, XACML or the Liberty Alliance's stack proposal it is comprehensible to see software developers often neglect the web service security part. Additionally, state-of-the-art IdM suites are just being prepared for WSOA [4]. As well, current application servers often do not yet support a necessary combination of relevant IdM standards to enable sophisticated access control. This is why as of today existing web services in most cases have little or no security features. Complications even increase when composing several web services which provide functionality from different underlying applications – workarounds like using the applications' built-in IdM are not applicable any more; an overall IdM architecture for WSOA is needed – enabling "identity as a service".

1.3 Contributions and Structuring of This Paper

The contributions of this paper are:

1. **The design of a service-oriented identity management architecture**, specified at service interfaces, the implementing components as well as the employed data repositories. The prerequisite is to respect WSOA-specifics like the loose coupling and the existence of basic and composite web services.

2. The alignment of the proposed architecture to existing and promising standards with the goal to **enable interoperability**.

The paper is organized as follows: section 2 introduces the architecture of WSOA and derives the requirements for appropriate IdM services building the bridging point between WSOA's core concerns and the IdM architecture. In section 3 we propose the design of a service-oriented identity management architecture and motivate how to gain interoperability. In section 4 we present our implementation experience. Section 5 treats the related work. A conclusion and an outlook on future work in this area close the body of the paper.

2 Web Service-Oriented Architecture and Requirements for Identity Management

The basic WSOA "layering" consists of existing applications at the bottom layer that are wrapped to web services, typically using application servers. Web services can be composed at an integration layer using BPEL. Web portals are used to integrate the (human) users using existing web technology like web browsers. The aforementioned further layers are put on top of the existing applications. Among others, this allows flexible service reuse in different business processes. This common core of WSOA can be found in many publications [5, 6, 7, 8]. It is important to notice that the web service architecture does not imply strict layering. Web services can be accessed either directly or via one or many intermediaries like BPEL engines. From WSOA's viewpoint the service interface of a BPEL-composed web service is not distinguishable from a basic one as they are both described using WSDL.

Before putting (web) service-oriented architectures to fly, there are fundamental questions to be answered: how is access control to be handled in this highly distributed and service-oriented environment? Slicing down existing applications to business related services, the internal IdM structures of the legacy systems are cut off. The alignment of the different system-specific IdM access control models and techniques with the goal to a local handling inside the applications complicates the integrated view on identity management. This is why the development of a WSOA-wide IdM architecture is favored. Being WSOA-aware itself, this infrastructure is meant to expose its functionality at service interfaces decoupling core concerns from IdM, especially access control. Following the paradigm of loose coupling and separation of concerns, the IdM part of WSOA's core concern services should be reduced to the bare minimum [9].

3 Design of a Service-Oriented Identity Management Architecture

From WSOA's perspective, the complexity of the IdM architecture is encapsulated at a set of service interfaces which should not have business domain-specific characteristics. The central goal of the IdM architecture is to verify authorization for service usage at runtime by enabling access control. Access control is based on two prerequisites: first, an authentication process checking any possible credentials has to be passed. This can be done once with validity for a series of subsequent accesses (relates to a single sign-on approach) or on every access – which is not favored in WSOA as there is usually a significant amount of services to be invoked. User authentication can be initiated at WSOA's portal layer for instance. Second, an authorization verification process is needed which checks if permission has been granted for the authenticated subject to invoke a WSOA service. The functionality of both (i.e. authentication and authorization verification) should be encapsulated at service interfaces featuring "identity as a service" for both basic and composite services. This implies that they simply hand over relevant data to the IdM services for calculation of access control.

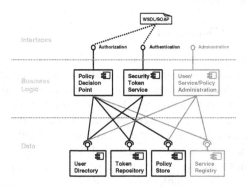

Fig. 1. Blueprint of a WSOA-aware IdM Architecture

In figure 1, we present the design of our web service-aware IdM architecture. There are three types of elements that are of interest: first, the IdM services towards WSOA's core concern part and towards administration. Second, the service implementing components and last but not least the data which the components operate on. In the following, we use this structuring to describe the design of our IdM architecture.

3.1 Interface Layer

Access control is based on authentication and implies authorization verification which typically are separate processes. Nowadays, access control is typically handled inside the system boundary of an application. In WSOA, the traditional application boundaries are put aside. Instead, web services are addressed exposing applications' core concerns. Following the concepts of "identity as a service", they import all functionality needed for access control using external service invocations.

Authentication is handled at the respective web service interface providing different operations to verify different types of credentials like username / password-based authentication, certificate-based authentication and so on. To enable single sign-on and to enhance privacy, a security token (establishing a session context) with WSOA-wide validity and the possibility for time-limitation is issued on successful authentication. User authentication can be initiated at WSOA's portal layer before accessing protected web services.

Authorization verification is based on an access control model. We have introduced an access control metamodel for web service-oriented architecture in [10] enhancing [11] and [12]. In short, for access control it is relevant to know which user is trying to access which web service operation and what the submitted invocations parameters are, as web services are defined at a high granularity. For the identification of the web service operation, they are all assigned a unique identifier. If a web service operation needs access control, it invokes the authorization verification service sending its identifier, the user's security token and the parameter the user had handed over. Using its internal policy data, the authorization verification service calculates a Boolean value which is returned and enables the web service to either proceed or stop operations.

The third interface of our IdM architecture is an administrative one. It is used to maintain the data as described later. It does not necessarily imply WSDL/SOAP, as administration is often done by humans.

3.2 Business Logic and Data Layer

The component implementing the authentication service is the *Security Token Service*. It takes user's identifier and corresponding credentials and does the verification. To protect users' privacy, we suggest issuing temporary security tokens on successful authentication. They are used as opaque handles towards user's identity which is thereby hidden to the core concern web services. Authentication is based on *User Directories*. Here the users, defined by their identifiers, credentials (e.g. passwords or certificates) along with their attributes are stored. The tuples of security token, user identifier and time limitation of the token are stored at the *Token Repository*.

Authorization verification is implemented at the *Policy Decision Point*. It takes the object identifier of the calling core concern operation, the user's security token and the operation's parameters and evaluates them using the corresponding access control policy which is deployed in the *Policy Store*. Here the information according to our WSOA access control metamodel is stored.

Besides identity management, there are further cross-cutting services like the WSOA's service registry. It is important to notice that it is implicitly linked to IdM: the *Service Registry* is used to store web services' descriptions whereas in the *Policy Store* the related policies are put. These two data repositories are linked using the web service operations' object identifiers that are assigned at deployment time. Thinking of relational databases, this identifier is analogous to foreign keys in WSOA's *Service Registry* and as a primary key in the *Policy Store*.

3.3 Enabling Interoperability

A major reason for the adoption of web-service oriented architecture is the interoperability which allows best of breed approaches with an easy integration of business functionality. WSDL [1] and SOAP [2] build the cornerstone for interoperability in WSOA, but the same challenges have to be fulfilled at the cross-cutting identity management architecture. We describe the authentication and authorization verification web service interfaces using WSDL and we apply SOAP communication with WS-Security-based message encryption between core concern web services and the IdM architecture [13]. After successful authentication, a SAML-conforming token (Security Assertion Markup Language, [14]) is issued to the user. The user is enabled to use his existing technology like his favored web browser as this token is mapped to a session cookie which is passed between the user's web browser and the web portal. At the portal this session cookie is mapped to a SAML token which is then piggybacked during all WSOA communication. As of now, there is a high interoperability problem if the security token of the user is sent in the SOAP header; this is why we put it in the SOAP body. The token in SOAP header is only used for point to point message encryption between participating web services. For the *Policy Enforcement Point* at the core concern part we use the design pattern *Secure Service Agent* as described in [15]. It handles the communication with the *Authorization Service* by sending the web service operation's identification, the user's SAML security token and the operation's parameters. We suggest using a relational database for the *Token Repository* and an LDAP-based *User Directory* where all users along with their attributes are stored. The *Policy Decision Point* applies a XACML component (eXtensible Access Control Markup Language, [16]) to verify authorization against XACML policies which are deployed at the *Policy Store*, in XACML contexts preferably using XML files. For WSOA's *Service Registry*, we suggest applying UDDI [17].

In figure 2 we depict on the left hand side the process of authentication and its involved parties using UML 2.0 sequence diagrams. Notice the gap between the *Portal* and the *Security Token Service* on the left hand and the *Policy Enforcement Point* and the *Policy Decision Point* on the right hand is the (virtual) border between WSOA's core concern part and the IdM architecture. Issuing security tokens and thereby establishing a session context enables the WSOA for single sign-on capabilities. On the right hand side the authorization verification process is depicted. The *Policy Enforcement Point* is a *Secure Service Agent* deployed once at every application server.

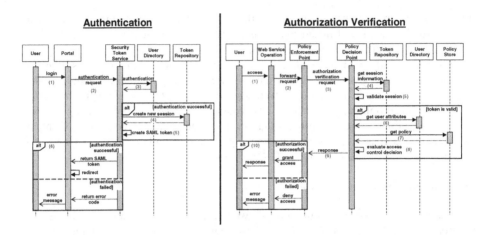

Fig. 2. Authentication and Authorization Verification Processes

4   Implementation Experience

We implemented the *Security Token Service* based on OpenSAML 1.1 [18]. The *Policy Decision Point* uses Sun's XACML 1.2 implementation [19]. Both components are realized as Enterprise Java Beans (EJB). To be deployable as web services, we used stateless session beans. The web service communication between core concern web services and the IdM services is encrypted using WS-Security [13]. Recognizing that application servers often do not support outbound encryption using the requester's key (JBoss, Oracle), we switched to BEA WebLogic 9.2 [20] which supports this necessary feature. The XACML policies are stored as XML files. To increase the performance, in a future release the policies will be stored in a relational database. The *User Directory* is realized using OpenLDAP 2.3. The *Token Repository* is stored in a relational database table using MySQL 5.0. We use SuSE Linux 10.1 as the operating system.

5   Related Work

There are several papers that address the core concern part of WSOA like the development of web services and their composition neglecting the aspect of access control, like [21, 22, 23]. They admit the necessity of identity management though they do not delve into it. On the other hand there are papers which explicitly address access control, but there they mostly focus on the implementation experience of a specific standard like XACML or SAML [24, 25, 26]. Additionally they lack the integrated view on the IdM architecture by focusing on either authentication or authorization and thereby do not support the concept of "identity as a service".

6   Conclusion and Further Work

In this paper we presented a blueprint for a service-oriented identity management architecture for web service environments. An authentication service issuing security tokens enables the web services for single sign-on. Our authorization verification service enables separation of concerns – the core concern web services apply access control via this loosely-coupled service. We have done a prototypical implementation securing our existing web services which we have summarized.

Our next steps are to consider a conjoint and model-driven development of web services with their associated access policies. Starting from computation-independent models at the business process level, they can be derived to platform-independent models and transformed to platform-specific models (i.e. IdM architecture-specific) which are effective calculable policies.

References

1. W3C: Web Services Description Language (WSDL) 1.1 (March 2001), http://www.w3.org/TR/wsdl
2. W3C: Simple Object Access Protocol (SOAP) 1.1 (May 2000), http://www.w3.org/TR/soap
3. Emig, C., Weisser, J., Abeck, S.: Development of SOA-Based Software Systems – an Evolutionary Programming Approach. In: IEEE Conference on Internet and Web Applications and Services ICIW'06, Guadeloupe / French Caribbean (February 2006)
4. Neuenschwander, M.: Enterprise Identity Management Market 2006–2007. Burton Group Identity and Privacy Strategies (November 2006)
5. Arsanjani, A.: Service-Oriented Modeling and Architecture, IBM developer works (2004)
6. Newcomer, E., Lomow, G.: Understanding SOA with Web Services. Addison Wesley Professional, Reading (December 2004)
7. Object Management Group (OMG): The OMG and Service Oriented Architecture, http://www.omg.org/attachments/pdf/OMG-and-the-SOA.pdf
8. Humm, B., Voss, M., Hess, A.: Rules for high-quality service-oriented Architectures (in German). Informatik Spektrum 29(6) (December 2006)
9. Burton Group: Directory Landscape – Directory Products evolve towards Identity Services, Version 1.0 (November 2004)
10. Emig, C., Brandt, F., Abeck, S., Biermann, J., Klarl, H.: An Access Control Metamodel for Web Service-Oriented Architecture (submitted for publication)
11. Yuan, E., Tong, J.: Attribute Based Access Control (ABAC) for Web Services. In: IEEE International Conference on Web Services (ICWS 2005), Orlando / Florida (July 2005)
12. Ferraiolo, D.F., Sandhu, R., Gavrila, S., Kuhn, D.R., Chandramouli, R.: Proposed NIST standard for role-based access control. ACM Transactions on Information and System Security (TISSEC) 4(3), 224–274 (2001)
13. Nadalin, A., Kaler, C., Monzillo, R., Hallam-Baker, P. (eds.): Web Services Security (WS-Security) Version 1.1 (February 2006)
14. OASIS Security Assertion Markup Language (SAML) 2.0 (2005), http://www.oasis-open.org/specs/index.php#samlv2.0
15. Emig, C., Schandua, H., Abeck, S.: SOA-aware Authorization Control. In: International Conference Software Engineering Advances ICSEA'06, Tahiti / French Polynesia (November 2006)
16. OASIS: eXtensible Access Control Markup Language (XACML) 2.0, http://www.oasis-open.org/committees/tc_home.php?wg_abbrev=xacml
17. OASIS: Universal Description, Discovery and Integration (UDDI) 3.0.2 (February 2005), http://www.oasis-open.org/committees/uddi-spec/doc/tcspecs.htm#uddiv3

18. OpenSAML - an Open Source Security Assertion Markup Language implementation: Project Homepage, http://www.opensaml.org
19. Sun's XACML Implementation: Project Homepage, http://sunxacml.sourceforge.net
20. BEA WebLogic Server® 9.2: Product Homepage, http://www.bea.com/framework.jsp? CNT=index.htm&FP=/content/products/weblogic/server/
21. Bosworth, A.: Developing Web Services. In: 17th International Conference on Data Engineering (2001)
22. Grønmo, R., Skogan, D., Solheim, I., Oldevik, J.: Model-driven Web Services Development. In: IEEE International Conference on e-Technology, e-Commerce and e-Service (2004)
23. Pasley, J.: How BPEL and SOA Are Changing Web Services Development. IEEE Internet Computing 9(3), 60–67 (2005)
24. Namli, T., Dogac, A.: Using SAML and XACML for Web Service Security & Privacy. Middle East Technical University, Ankary / Turkey (2007)
25. Tao, H.: A XACML-based Access Control Model for Web Service. In: IEEE Conference on Wireless Communications, Networking and Mobile Computing (2005)
26. Peng, Y., Wu, Q.: Secure Communication and Access Control for Web Services Container. In: 5th International Conference on Grid and Cooperative Computing (2006)

Towards a Context Binding Transparency[*]

Tom Broens, Dick Quartel, and Marten van Sinderen

Center for Telematics and Information Technology, ASNA group, University of Twente,
P.O. Box 217, 7500 AE Enschede, The Netherlands
{t.h.f.broens, d.a.c.quartel, m.j.vansinderen}@utwente.nl
http://asna.ewi.utwente.nl

Abstract. Context-aware applications use context information, like location or identification of nearby objects of interest, to adapt their behavior to the current situation of the user. These applications acquire context information from distributed context sources, like GPS receivers and RFID beacons. Consequently, context-aware applications must be able to discover, select and bind to suitable context sources. Furthermore, due to the dynamic nature of context sources, their (lasting) availability is not guaranteed and the quality of their context information may vary. This makes maintaining a context binding – i.e., a binding between a context source and an application - complex. In this paper, we propose a context binding transparency that simplifies creating and maintaining a context binding. The proposed solution encompasses a language to specify context requirements and offerings, and interfaces to retrieve the requested context information. The responsibility for discovery, selection, binding and maintenance of required bindings is delegated to our underlying middleware, coined CACI. By providing this context binding transparency, we reduce the required development effort for creating context-aware applications.

1 Introduction

The user's environment is increasingly equipped with a multitude of devices, ranging from laptops and mobile phones to Internet connected refrigerators. In the vision of ubiquitous computing [1], these devices should cooperate to unobtrusively offer relevant services to users. 'Unobtrusiveness' is defined by the Merriam-Webster dictionary as not being obtrusive, meaning not being undesirably prominent[1]. In relation to ubiquitous computing this means that, amongst others, offered services should take the current situation of the user into account to tailor the behavior to that situation. For example, when a telephone call comes in and a user cannot be disturbed, his phone will not ring but vibrate.

A way to enable unobtrusive services is context-aware computing [2]. Context-aware applications take besides explicit user input also the situation of an entity (i.e. person, place or object relevant to the functioning of the application) into account, to

---

[*] This work is part of the Freeband AWARENESS Project. Freeband is sponsored by the Dutch government under contract BSIK 03025. (http://awareness.freeband.nl)
[1] http://www.m-w.com/dictionary/obtrusive

A. Pras and M. van Sinderen (Eds.): EUNICE 2007, LNCS 4606, pp. 9–16, 2007.
© Springer-Verlag Berlin Heidelberg 2007

provide tailored functionality. Common examples of context information are user location and presence, temperature of a room and available communication bandwidth. Context-awareness is particularly interesting for mobile applications, because these type of applications function in constantly changing environments. For example, a mobile tourist guide application could benefit from context by offering personalized tourist information based on the current physical location of the user.

Generally, a context-aware system consists of software components that can have the following two roles: context producer and context consumer. Context producers acquire context information from the environment and make it available to context consumers. For example, a software component that can offer the location provided by GPS receivers or RFID beacons. We call these software components context sources. A context consumer retrieves context information from a context producer. Typically, a context-aware application fulfills a context consumer role. However, a context-aware application can also be a context producer when its application logic creates context information. For a context-aware application to use context information, it has to associate with a suitable context source. We call this association a context binding.

In first generation context-aware applications context bindings were hard coded inside the application logic [3]. This leads to fixed couplings between context-aware applications and specific context sources, resulting in inflexible applications that cannot cope with changing circumstances and future evolutions. Currently, there is a trend towards middleware infrastructures for context-aware applications [4]. These infrastructures offer solutions to recurring problems like context discovery, adaptation and security. However, some key challenges remain, driven by the inherent characteristics of context sources: (i) context information can be offered by a multitude of physically distributed context sources. Problems that arise are how-to find relevant context sources and how to easily bind to these remote context sources, (ii) (similar) context sources can be provided by different context providers using different data models for storing and accessing context information. Problems that arise are how-to create interoperability between context sources, (iii) context sources have fluctuating properties. First, they can appear and disappear at arbitrary moment. Secondly, their quality, which is called Quality of Context (QoC)[5], can vary among context sources and also among context samples provided by context sources.

Without supporting mechanisms, coping with these challenges is hard for application developers. Creating and maintaining context bindings requires substantial development effort. In this paper, we propose a context binding transparency that provides means to simplify the development of creating and maintaining context bindings. This transparency encompasses a language to specify context requirements and offerings (see [6]), and interfaces to retrieve the requested context information. The responsibility for discovery, selection, binding and maintenance of required context bindings is shifted to our underlying middleware context binding mechanisms, coined CACI. By providing this context binding transparency, we reduce the required development effort for creating context-aware applications.

In this paper, we focus on the high-level design aspects of our context binding transparency to position it in the overall development of context-aware applications. In comparison, in [6] and [7] we take a more bottom-up approach describing the detailed design of our underlying context binding mechanisms (CACI), the context requirement language and proof-of-concept implementation.

The remainder of this paper is structured as follows: Section 2 discusses a basic model of context-aware applications, which forms the framework to position our proposed binding transparency. Furthermore, it is used to identify involved functions relevant for the design of our binding transparency. Section 3 continues by describing the high-level design of our binding transparency. Section 4 briefly discusses our proof-of-concept implementation and evaluation. In Section 5, we present some conclusions and directions for future work.

2 Model of Context-Aware Applications

Since the 1980's, context-awareness has gained momentum in the ubiquitous computing, pervasive computing and ambient intelligence research communities. Context is defined as any information that characterizes the situation of an entity (i.e. user, place or computational object) relevant to the application behavior [2]. Examples of context are location, presence, temperature, number of emails, conversation partner etc. We define context-aware applications as applications that adapt their default behavior to the context at hand.

Context-aware applications are characterized by the use of context inputs additional to user input. Optionally, context-aware applications can produce context, which can be made available to the environment (for example to other context-aware applications). Therefore, context-aware applications can also act as context sources when they produce and output context. Figure 1 illustrates these characteristics.

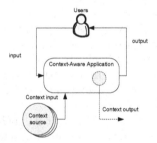

Fig. 1. Context-aware application

We consider context-aware applications as an extension of non-context-aware applications. Context-aware applications have a basic non-context-aware behavior, which is adapted when context is used. We assume that a context-aware application can function without context but can do its job better when considering context.

Let us consider the previous intuitive notion on context-aware application and discuss it from a modeling point of view. We start with a high-level black-box description of a context-aware application and its supporting context middleware (see Figure 2).

A context-aware application uses context to adapt its behavior. Furthermore, it can produce context. We consider a context middleware that facilitates these needs by offering a context retrieval and context publishing service. The context retrieval service facilitates the context-aware application to retrieve context. The context publishing service facilitates the context-aware application to publish its context to the environment.

The context-aware application in itself can be further detailed into two main functional elements: application logic and context logic (see Figure 3). Application logic is the behavior of the application (that fulfils the users need), which is influenced by context information and possibly can produce context. Context logic is the behavior needed for the application logic to retrieve its required context information or publish its offered context information.

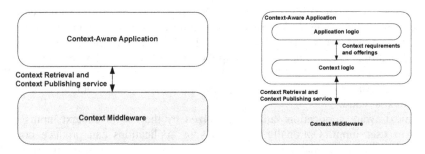

Fig. 2. & Fig. 3. Zooming into context-aware applications

When zooming into the context logic (see Figure 4), two functional elements can be distinguished. First, the context consumer element consists of behavior to retrieve context required by the application logic. For an application to be context-aware, it requires to have context consumer functionality. The context producer element is optional and consists of behavior to publish the offered context of the application logic. In this paper, we also use the term context consumer and producer role. With this we indicate that a context-aware application consist of a context consumer and respectively context producer element.

Both the context retrieval service and the context publishing service are provided by the context middleware. We denote the specific middleware functionality that provides these services as context management. Context middleware may also consist of other elements like communication and security mechanisms. These are out of the scope of the model presented in this paper.

We model context sources similarly to context-aware applications (see Figure 5). It consists of application logic responsible for sensing, acquiring and processing context into context offerings. The context logic has a mandatory context producer function that is responsible for publishing offered context produced by the application logic.

As you can see, a context-aware application A can appear as a context source for context-aware application B that is using the context of context-aware application A. However, there also exist non-context-aware applications that are context sources. They have as sole purpose producing context. For example, an application part that wraps a GPS to produce location information.

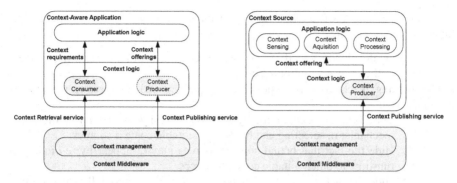

Fig. 4. & Fig. 5. Zooming into context-aware applications and context sources

Figure 6 shows the relationship between a context consumer (i.e. context-aware application) and a context producer (i.e. context source). For a context consumer to retrieve context it needs a binding with a context producer. Our binding transparency hides physical context producers and provides ways, via interactions with the context middleware for context consumers to create and maintain context bindings. The application developer of a context-aware application (context consumer) is unaware of the context producer with which a binding is created, how this binding is created and how this binding is maintained to overcome the dynamicity of context producers. The next section discusses this context binding transparency in more detail.

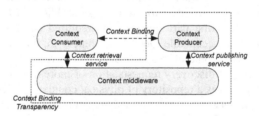

Fig. 6. Relation between context consumer and context producer

3   High-Level Design of a Context Binding Transparency

The concept of transparencies was introduced in the context of distributed system in the Open Distributed Processing (ODP) reference model [8]. Transparencies are mechanisms that hide certain complexities for the application developer to simplify the development of their application. For example, location transparency [8] masks out the problems of locating distributed objects by enabling them to be found using logical names rather than physical addresses.

We propose a binding transparency that hides the complexities of developing context-aware applications dealing with creating and maintaining context bindings. When re-considering figure 4, our binding transparency can be positioned between the context-aware application and the context middleware offering a specific instance of the context retrieval and publishing service. Due to space limitations, we focus in this paper on the context retrieval service. Key features of our proposed transparency (i.e. for context retrieval) are:

- Application developers specify their context requirement in a context requirement language rather than programming code.
- Our binding mechanism is responsible for parsing and interpreting the context requirements to:
  - o Initialize a context binding by discovering (using an underlying discovery mechanism), selecting and binding to suitable context sources.
  - o Hide the fact that bound context sources may disappear by re-binding at run-time to other suitable context sources.
  - o Hide the fact that the QoC of the context sources may fall below a speci-fied level by re-binding at run-time to other suitable context sources.
  - o Re-bind to context sources with a higher QoC when they become avail-able.
- Supporting interoperability of different available underlying context discovery mechanisms.
- Offering a uniform interface to retrieve context information without being aware of the heterogeneity of physical context source.

Figure 7 presents the internal perspective of the context retrieval service showing functional elements and their interaction. A context-aware application with its specific application logic formulates some context requirements (i.e. specified by the applica-tion developer) (1). These are translated into in one or more binding creation requests by the context logic and transferred to the context middleware (2). These requests consist of two parts. The first part specifies the required context information. The second part specifies the acceptable QoC. The context middleware in terms of the context retriever stores the binding requests and tries to resolve the context require-ments by invoking context discovery requests at on or more available context manag-ers (3). A context manager is a repository of physical context sources (4) which offers a context discovery service. This service enables context-aware applications to find context sources that can offer specified context.

The context logic of the application can use the context retrieval service to retrieve context in a (i) request-response and (ii) subscribe-notify manner. The subscription mechanism is controlled by application specified subscription criteria (e.g. periodical updates, updates when the context information changes, updates based on criteria that are more complex).

When an established binding fails (e.g. application out of range of the sensors) or new context sources (i.e. other QoC) become available, the middleware will try to (re)establish a suitable binding. When this is not possible, the context-aware applica-tion is notified. When the application does not require any context anymore, for ex-ample because it quits, it can notify the middleware to destroy the established binding.

When a binding creation request is invoked by the context-aware application, the context retriever creates a context producer proxy (CP'') (5) which acts as the single point of access to context used by the application. This context retriever discovers and selects a suitable context producer (CP*, reference of a context source (CS)). The CP'' is bound to the selected CP* (6). From this moment the CP'' can deliver context to the context-aware application. When a binding destroy request is invoked by the context-aware application the CP'' is unbound to the CP* and is cleaned-up from the context retriever administration.

Recapitalizing, from the perspective of the application, the physical context sources and their dynamicity are hidden. The application interacts with the context middleware to retrieve context rather than with individual context sources.

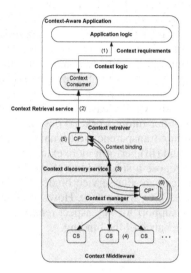

Fig. 7. Context retrieval binding transparency

4 Implementation and Evaluation

In [6] and [7], we discuss more details on our underlying context middleware (CACI) and our proof-of-concept implementation. The implementation is based on Java and the OSGi component framework. The language to express context requirements is based on XML. The prototype is tested on a regular PC using a standard VM and a mobile device running the IBM J9 virtual machine. For testing, we create a component generator that can generate and deploy a template component with a user-defined context requirements document. SimuContext [9], a framework to simulate context sources, is used as the underlying context discovery mechanism.

Preliminary evaluation of our binding transparency using the implemented proof-of-concept (see [7]) showed a decrease of programming effort, needed to create and maintain bindings, from approximately 1000 to 60 lines of code. The learning curve to use our transparency is limited due to the simple XML-based context requirement specification language and straightforward interfaces. Furthermore, without our transparency also the underlying discovery mechanisms have to be learned. Preliminary performance evaluations, performed by inserting probes in the proof-of-concept, showed neglectable (< 1ms) overhead for establishing a binding, for instance compared to remote invocation of a context discovery mechanism, introduced by the binding mechanisms.

5   Conclusion

This paper discusses a model of context-aware applications and focuses on the design aspects of our proposed binding transparency. We take the perspective of the application developer and aim, with this transparency, to hide the complexity of creating and maintaining context bindings, needed for context-aware applications to retrieve context information. We propose a context retrieval service that implements this transparency. This service has as goal to offer the 'best possible' context to the service user during the existence of a context binding. With the 'best possible' context, we mean: (i) guaranteed continuity of available context information when possible and (ii) deliver context information that has the highest possible quality of context. Initial evaluations, by applying the transparency in applications develop in the AWARENESS project have shown the feasibility of our approach. However, several aspects need to be tackled in our future work: (i) design of the context providing service, (ii) extending the binding transparency to (dynamically) interoperate with multiple discovery mechanisms and (iii) perform more extensive performance evaluations.

Other approaches that propose a similar kind of mechanism that uses a specification language to bind services are the service binder [10] and the extended service binder [11] proposed for the OSGi framework. However, they focus on generic OSGi services and therefore lack support for key aspect required for context exchange like quality of context and maintenance of the binding.

References

[1] Weiser, M.: The Computer for the Twenty-First Century. Scientific American, pp. 94–110 (September 1991)
[2] Dey, A.: Providing Architectural Support for Context-Aware applications. PhD thesis, Georgia Institute of Technology (2000)
[3] Korkea-aho, M.: Context-Aware Applications Survey (2000), http://users.tkk.fi/~mkorkeaa/doc/context-aware.html
[4] Henricksen, K., Indulska, J., McFadden, T., Balasubramaniam, S.: Middleware for Distributed Context-Aware Systems. In: DOA 2005, Agia Napa, Cyprus (2005)
[5] Buchholz, T., Kupper, A., Schiffers, M.: Quality of Context: What it is and why we need it. In: HPOVUA 2003, Geneva, Switzerland (2003)
[6] Broens, T., Halteren, A., Sinderen, M.v.: Infrastructural Support for Dynamic Context Bindings. In: Havinga, P., Lijding, M., Meratnia, N., Wegdam, M. (eds.) EuroSSC 2006. LNCS, vol. 4272, Springer, Heidelberg (2006)
[7] Broens, T., Sinderen, M.v., Halteren, A., Quartel, D.: Dynamic Context Bindings in Pervasive Middleware. In: Middleware Support for Pervasive Computing Workshop (PerWare'07), White Plains, USA (2007)
[8] Blair, G., Stefani, J.: Open Distributed Processing and Multimedia. Addison-Wesley, Reading (1998)
[9] Broens, T., van Halteren, A.: SimuContext: simulating context sources for context-aware applications. In: Presented at Intl. Conference on Networking and Services (ICNS06), Silicon Valley, USA (2006)
[10] Cervantas, H., Hall, R.: Autonomous Adaptation to Dynamic Availability Using a Service-Oriented Component Model. In: ICSE 2006, Edinburgh, Scotland (2004)
[11] Bottaro, A., Gerodolle, A.: Extended Service Binder: Dynamic Service Availability Management in Ambient Intelligence. In: FRCSS 2006, Vienna, Austria (2006)

A Context Middleware Using an Ontology-Based Information Model

Iris Hochstatter[1], Michael Duergner[2], and Michael Krause[3]

[1] Munich Network Management Team, Information Systems Laboratory (IIS),
University of Federal Armed Forces Munich, 85577 Neubiberg, Germany
`Iris.Hochstatter@unibw.de`
[2] Ludwig-Maximilians-Universität München
`Michael.Duergner@stud.ifi.lmu.de`
[3] BearingPoint, München
`Michael.Krause@ifi.lmu.de`

Abstract. For the adaptation of services to the current situation of a user, the services are in need of specific context information. The acquisition of context in highly dynamic environments is a complex process as the appropriate context sources are not known in advance. Moreover, to realize Mark Weiser's vision of ubiquitous computing, many services on the one hand and a good deal of context information on the other hand have to be combined. Hence, we follow a middleware approach to automate context retrieval for services. For the exchange over domain boundaries, services in need of and services offering context information have to agree on a common description of the information. Therefore, a flexible and extensible information model is a basic requirement. This paper describes in detail the integration of those two important foundations of context-aware computing.

1 Introduction

In highly dynamic environments with a multitude of mobile entities, it is important for (i) context-aware services to find and for (ii) context information services to provide context information to many other systems. A restaurant finder service for example looks for venues close to the user's location and may depend on many other information describing the user's situation. Which context information services, i.e. context sources it has to query will not be known until the actual query is made. On the other hand, context information about any entity, as for example the user's location can be used in many different context-aware services. To relieve context-aware services of the intricacies of context retrieval and composition as well as to facilitate the reuse of context information at the same time, in [1] we proposed infra-structural services, namely the CoCo Infrastructure. Context information is exchanged over domain boundaries, thus all involved actors have to agree on how to express and interpret context information. Therefore, an information model has to balance expressiveness and inferential efficiency. In [2] we introduced a modeling approach based on ontologies that takes into account the special characteristics of context information.

A. Pras and M. van Sinderen (Eds.): EUNICE 2007, LNCS 4606, pp. 17–24, 2007.

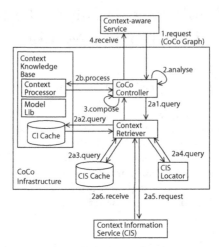

Fig. 1. Middleware: The CoCo infrastructure

In this paper we will go into details about the integration of this ontology-based information model into our context middleware.

The paper is structured as follows: section 2 and 3 presents the basic building blocks CoCo Infrastructure and Context Meta-Model. Section 4 discusses the integration of the ontology-based information model into the context middleware. We conclude the paper with a short summary and an outlook to future work.

2   The CoCo Infrastructure

The *CoCo Infrastructure* (see fig. 1) acts as a broker between context-aware services (CAS) that request context information and context information services (CIS) that provide context information. It therefore relieves the context-aware services from the burden of discovering context information services, data transformation, or derivation of high-level context information from low-level context information.

CoCo stands for *Composing Context*. The CoCo Infrastructure does not only support the request for a single piece of context information (like 'the current position of Alex') but also the request for composed context information (like 'the temperature at the place where Alex currently is'). This requires the ability to describe such compositions. Therefore, we have developed a language that describes the request for composed context information in so-called CoCo graphs [1]. The graph-like structures are expressed in XML.

Basically a CoCo Graph is made out of two types of nodes: *Factory Nodes* describing the requested piece of context information and *Operator Nodes* containing instructions how to process one or several pieces of context information. The procedure is as follows: (step 1) First, the request in form of a CoCo graph, is sent from the context-aware service to the CoCo infrastructure where it is (step 2) analyzed by the *CoCo Controller*.

For every Factory Node it sends (step 2a1) a request for context information to the *Context Retriever*, which at first queries the *Context Cache* (step 2a2), whether it already has got the requested information. In case it is not available there, the *CIS Cache* is asked whether it already knows an appropriate context information service to retrieve the information from (step 2a3). If not it then instructs the *CIS Locator* to find appropriate context information services (step 2a4), to which the retriever sends related context requests. After having received context information for each request (step 2a5 and step 2a6) the retriever matches this information against the request of the controller, selects the most appropriate piece of context information and returns it to the controller.

For each Operator Node, the controller instructs the *Context Processor* to execute its operation (step 2b), e.g. adaptation, selection or aggregation. Context Processor and Context Cache are part of the *Context Knowledge Base*, which also includes the *Model Lib*. The Model Lib contains the ontology-based information model the middleware is based upon, this will be discussed in the next section.

3   The Context Meta-Model

To facilitate a common understanding and a uniform representation of context, we developed an information model as foundation for context interoperability. This model was introduced in [2]. Context information poses special requirements on an information model as literally every information can be used as context information. It is therefore not sufficient to have a single context model but we propose a Context Meta-Model (CMM) that can be used by application developers to design their own application specific context models, reuse existing models and combine both possibilities. We base our information model on ontologies and thus gain the possibility to perform reasoning and an important formal basis. Description logics are a set of logic-based formalisms used to specify ontologies. They identify a subset of first order logic that offers a good trade-off between expressiveness on the one hand and determinable and efficient inference on the other. To account for flexibility, the CMM incorporates rules that are based on Horn formulae.

Basic building blocks for representing (context) knowledge in our context meta-model are entity classes, datatype classes, and properties with their associated quality classes (see figure 2):

- *Entity class*: base construct for representing a group of entities (persons, places, things, events etc.) that belong together because they share some properties
- *Datatype class*: base construct for representing a datatype (temperature, noise level, position etc.)
- *Property*: base construct for representing a type of relationship between an instance of an entity class and an instance of either an entity or a dataype class. An example for a *property* as a relation between two entities on the

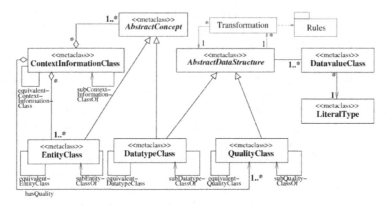

Fig. 2. The Context Meta-Model

model layer is: **Person** "owns" **MobilePhone**. **Person** "hasPhoneNumber" **PhoneNumber** relates an entity with a datatype (more details are given in the next subsection).

- *Quality class*: base construct for representing specific quality aspects of dynamically acquired information (certainty, precision, resolution etc.) also known as *Quality of Context*.

In order to represent *temporal history* information, for every property the acquisition time is captured as a timestamp. It is a mandatory quality class for every property. *Dependencies* between properties are expressed as rules in the form of Horn clauses. Each rule expresses an implication between an antecedent and consequent: whenever the conditions specified in the antecedent hold, the conditions specified in the successor must also hold. This allows to specify consistency conditions as well as derivation rules. Conditions can reference entity classes and datatype classes as well as properties and their associated quality classes. This way a rule can take into account quality information and also specify the quality of the deduced properties.

In addition, there are two special constructs for the semantically rich specification of datatypes: datavalue properties and transformation rules. A *Datavalue Class* is a base construct for specifying data structures, i.e. datatype classes and quality classes. Each datavalue class associates a data structure (*Abstract-DataStructure*) with a literal type and thus allows to compose complex data structures from literals. E.g. the coordinates for a position are composed from **longitude** and **latitude**. The *Transformation* is the base construct for representing a transformation from values of one data structure to values of another data structure. An example is the transformation between a position in Gauss-Krueger coordinates into a WGS-84 format, the transformation function itself is given or described in form of a rule on class level in the *Rules* and the identifier for the rule is given in the model itself.

Further modeling constructs are *specialization-relations* that may be specified between two classes of the same kind in order to organize them in (separate) specialization hierarchies. Finally, there are *equivalence-relations*. Their semantics is that the first node represents the equivalent concept or role as the second node and should therefore be interpreted equivalently. They are useful for mapping context models that have been developed separately in order to enable interoperability.

4 Integrating the Context Meta-Model into the CoCo Infrastructure

As context information services and context-aware services as well as a context composition middleware will be operated by different providers, who may not even know each other directly, the main goal behind the implementation was to enable the use of different context models nearly automatically to facilitate interoperability. This can only be achieved if the middleware does not care about the specific context model it deals with at the moment. CoCo itself operates in most parts just within the structure given by the context meta model (CMM). This allows an easy integration of new context models into CoCo on-the-fly at runtime without even stopping the service. Furthermore it should enable us to delegate the retrieval of context model specific code to either a third-party service or maybe even use in Java integrated mechanism.

The identification of a specific context model and `EntityClass` or `ContextInformationClass` of this model is performed on the XML layer by the namespace and the name of the XML tag, i.e. by its qualified name. The Model Lib of CoCo therefore has an integrated mechanism to translate this qualified name into a Java package name and class name to actually load the correct Plain Old Java Object (POJO). The only prerequisite for this to work is, that the needed classes have to be within the classpath of the CoCo service. This is right now done by copying the JAR packages there but should be replaced by the possibility to automatically load the classes via the Internet directly from the vendor's location.

In this section, we will first give a detailed view on the process that is executed in the CoCo middleware, we then describe the integration of the ontology-based information model CMM into the CoCo Infrastructure and show the achievements of this work.

4.1 Parsing and Binding

The first action that takes place when the service is invoked is that it tries to parse the submitted CoCo Graph and determines if it is syntactically and semantically correct, as far as CoCo is able to understand the semantics. Parsing is done in a two step approach, i.e. in the first step we create a DOM tree out of the XML document and do the syntax checks here. The second one is to parse this DOM tree and translate the elements to the appropriate POJOs, e.g. a factory-node DOM element creates a FactoryNode Java object. Afterwards one of the most important actions takes place, i.e. the different Input-, Factory-,

Operator- and OutputNodes are bound to each other according to the dependencies specified by the user. E.g. the Factory Node which is responsible to retrieve the temperature for the location where Axel is, is bound to the Factory Node which gets Alex's location as this location is a prerequesite for the other one.

As Factory Nodes normally are just bound to one other node OperatorNodes may be bound to a theoretically nearly infinite number of other nodes. Due to the structure of Operator Nodes there are also bindings within the OperatorNode itself, e.g. the output of an Operator Node may be the outcome of a calculation done inside the node or may be a fixed value depending on the outcome of the calculation. The power and possibilities of Operator Nodes are not completely visible at the moment as they depend closely on the context models available.

4.2   Starting and Running the Nodes

After the binding step is complete the CoCo Controller searches for these nodes which are not bound to any other and starts them. Afterwards, the Node tries to fulfill its task, i.e. either invoke the CoCo Retriever to fetch context information in case of a Factory Node or to hand over to the CoCo Processor in case of an Operator Node. In both cases the involved components report either the sucessful execution or any error to the Node which has invoked them. In case of success the result is returned, i.e. the outcome of the operation or the retrieved context, and the Node is then responsible to inform all nodes which are bound to it about the fulfillment of the task. If an error occured during execution, e.g. if there is no way to retrieve the requested context information for whatever reasons, the Node is responsible to inform the CoCo Controller about this problem which afterwards has to deal with this issue.

This mechanism goes on as long as there are any nodes left that need to be executed. In case the node is an OutputNode it either has the value already in case of a fixed value, or it retrieves it from the node it is bound to and informs the CoCo Controller that it is ready to return its value. After all output nodes have reported to the CoCo Controller it is its task to compose the XML document which is returned to the user.

4.3   Integrating Jena with the CoCo Infrastructure

The Jena framework [3] is a Java framework for developing Semantic Web [4] applications. It implements the modeling languages RDF, RDFS and OWL, and provides a rule-based inference engine. The Jena database system [5] uses the JDBC to connect to a relational database like MySQL, Oracle or PostgreSQL. RDF triples are stored with subject, predicate and object and each line corresponds to one RDF statement. Jena allows to manage different RDF models simultaneously by assigning an own triple table to each of the models. Jena also includes a SPARQL engine (SPARQL Protocol And RDF Query Language) [6]. SPARQL is a data-oriented query language that searches the model and returns relevant information as a graph or a set of variables. Its syntax is similar to an SQL statement and supports four different request types. Jena is therefore well suited for introducing our semantic information model to the CoCo Infrastructure and allows us to store context information persistently in a database while retaining the semantics as it supports OWL DL.

To integrate Jena with the CoCo Infrastructure, we added an interface `ContextInformationCacheJena` to the CoCo Infrastructure that includes the procedures `insert` and `query`. The Jena database subsystem uses the JDBC driver to connect to a PostgreSQL database. After connecting to the database, a persistent model has to be created with the `ModelFactory`. Whenever the Context Retriever receives a request for context information, it first queries the Context Cache via the new interface. The `query` procedure proceeds in five steps: First, from a list of all available models the appropriate has to be chosen and opened. Next, an ontology model is created from the model: the ontology model also contains specification information regarding the ontology language, reasoner and storage location. A SPARQL query searches for the entity and its relevant context. As an entity can have multiple identities, it has to be looked for each of them. When the right entity has been found according to its identity, the sought-after context information can be retrieved in a next step. The result is a model, that has to be converted to a DOM element. Usually the DOM parser should be able to convert the model to a DOM element. Unfortunately, the parser could not resolve namespaces, so in our case the `query` procedure calls a conversion procedure and the model is first converted to a JDOM element and then to a DOM element. The DOM element is finally returned to the Context Retriever.

If the query fails because the context information was not in the Context Cache, the Context Retriever looks for an adequate context information service and queries it. The response is then stored in the Context Cache via the insert procedure. The `insert` procedure has an `EntityClass` object as parameter. This object is first converted to a DOM object and then stored as an RDF model in the database.

5   Related Work

Various approaches to infrastructural support of CASs as well as to context modeling exist. In previous works on those topics, existing approaches to context provisioning (cp. [1]) and context information models (cp. [7] and [8]) have been evaluated thoroughly. In this paper, we present only the most important findings from this extensive research regarding the modeling of context information. In terms of expressiveness, there is no approach that captures all features of context information so far. Most of the existing approaches restrict their generality by stipulating semantic categories and almost none provide constructs to express meta information which is crucial to determine whether the given context information is useful for a particular service. Many of the approaches, in particular earlier ones, lack a formal foundation that is necessary to enable efficient inference, extensibility and distribution of models. In addition, support for interoperability is not explicitly given. Shortcomings in terms of expressiveness and structure result in difficult applicability of an approach in practice.

6   Conclusion

The complex task of brokering context information between all involved actors has been discussed in this paper. Based on the description of a middleware and an ontology-based information model, the concrete integration of both has been described in great detail. Due to the combination of relatively new technologies it has to be dealt with unexpected challenges but the approach shows the feasibility and with proceeding development, the advantages will be even more substantial.

Though this conceptual change in the CoCo Infrastructure works quite well there remains room for improvement. At the moment, context information is stored in the database but never erased or moved. While historical context information surely is useful, databases will get out of hand without a fitting algorithm to clear the database possibly relying on the Quality of Context. Secondly, with the improvement of OWL databases and inference engines a lot more efficient solutions will be possible.

Acknowledgments. The authors wish to thank the members of the Munich Network Management (MNM) Team for helpful discussions and valuable comments. The MNM Team founded by Prof. Dr. Heinz-Gerd Hegering is a group of researchers of the University of Munich, the Munich University of Technology, the University of Federal Armed Forces Munich and the Leibniz Supercomputing Centre of the Bavarian Academy of Sciences. Its web-server is located at http://www.mnm-team.org. This work has been performed partially in the framework of the EU IST Network of Excellence EMANICS Management of Internet Technologies and Complex Services (IST-NoE-026854).

References

1. Buchholz, T., Krause, M., Linnhoff-Popien, C., Schiffers, M.: CoCo: Dynamic Composition of Context Information. In: Proceedings of the First Annual International Conference on Mobile and Ubiquitous Computing (MobiQuitous) (August 2004)
2. Fuchs, F., Hochstatter, I., Krause, M., Berger, M.: A Meta–Model Approach to Context Information. In: Proceedings of 2nd IEEE PerCom Workshop on Context Modeling and Reasoning (CoMoRea) (at 3rd IEEE International Conference on Pervasive Computing and Communication (PerCom 2005)) (March 2005)
3. Jena Semantic Web Framework, http://jena.sourceforge.net/
4. World Wide Web Consortium: Semantic Web, http://www.w3.org/2001/sw/
5. Wilkinson, K., Sayers, C., Kuno, H., Reynolds, D.: Efficient RDF Storage and Retrieval in Jena2. In: Aberer, K., Koubarakis, M., Kalogeraki, V. (eds.) Databases, Information Systems, and Peer-to-Peer Computing. LNCS, vol. 2944, pp. 131–150. Springer, Heidelberg (2004)
6. World Wide Web Consortium: SPARQL Query Language for RDF
7. Fuchs, F.: A Modeling Technique for Context Information Master's Thesis, Ludwig Maximilian University Munich (2004)
8. Strang, T., Linnhoff-Popien, C.: A Context Modeling Survey. In: Proceedings of the Workshop on Advanced Context Modeling, Reasoning and Management (2004)

Providing Movement Information to Applications in Wireless IPv6 and Mobile IPv6 Terminals

Jarno Kalliomäki, Bilhanan Silverajan, and Jarmo Harju

Institute of Communications Engineering,
Tampere University of Technology,
P.O. Box 553,
33101 Tampere Finland
firstname.lastname@tut.fi

Abstract. Innovative, adaptive and context-aware applications today are poised to take advantage of their immediate surroundings for interaction, both with the user as well as with other surrounding devices. Often, these applications reside in mobile devices, and the need for obtaining movement detection information is placed at a premium. However, very little work actually exists in bringing this information to such applications in a uniform way. In this paper, we address the lack of consistent application level support for obtaining timely information related to network-level movement detection and location awareness, by presenting the design and architecture of a movement notification system to support advanced mobile applications. This system was designed primarily for use for wireless devices moving in IPv6 and Mobile IPv6 spaces, although it can also be used for IPv4. Future work on the system is also discussed.

Keywords: Movement Detection, Mobile Computing, IPv6.

1 Introduction

Future wireless and pervasive computing environments are envisaged to support the ability for a diverse range of portable wireless peripherals to roam seamlessly across different wireless networks. The gradual development of higher wireless data rates in the next few years, and the proliferation of mobile devices such as laptops, phones and PDAs, point to a distant but realistic possibility: the emergence of networks which only need a wired infrastructure for access points, switches, routers, aggregators and other network elements, but not to the devices themselves. Everything ranging from video streaming to VoIP, seamless and transparent handovers between WiFi and 3G networks and location-based services are being touted as killer applications for these devices.

IPv6 and Mobile IPv6 will be the most likely technologies to drive the deployment for such future networks. IPv6 offers automatic address configuration, and lifts the NAT tax by supplying a global address space supporting billions of unique hosts. With the inclusion of IPsec, end-to-end reachability can be securely obtained. With Mobile IPv6, mobile terminals can always remain reachable via home addresses, independent of their location, but also receive temporary Care-Of Addresses.

A. Pras and M. van Sinderen (Eds.): EUNICE 2007, LNCS 4606, pp. 25–32, 2007.

This extra degree of mobility and the desire for seamless connectivity will give rise to new breeds of network applications and services no longer relying on traditional abstractions that Internet services have long been modeled on. The proper functioning of these applications might depend on information gathered from the immediate vicinity though often, when roaming into network spaces for the first time they will have no previous knowledge of the types of services and other devices resident in the new network space. Also, network attachment points may change when the devices discover new access networks or lose connectivity to previously attached networks.

Therefore, one of the primary issues in developing such advanced applications is to address the lack of consistent application level support for obtaining timely information related to network-level movement detection and location awareness, which may be inherently and readily available at the local interfaces of these devices.

This paper highlights our activities in raising the importance of supporting rapid movement detection as an underlying foundation for the development of advanced mobile applications, and the importance of exporting this information for use in a consistent manner that may reside in these devices. A movement notification system named Mobinfo was designed and implemented to support advanced mobile applications.

Section 2 provides a quick survey of how movement notification can benefit different classes of applications. Section 3 provides a detailed design of Mobinfo. Section 4 outlines the future direction of work with our movement notification system, and Section 5 draws some conclusions.

2 Movement Notification: Usage Scenarios

Movement detection and notification would prove beneficial to many classes of applications. Some of these are described in the following paragraphs.

Mobile applications running in Mobile IPv6 mobile nodes would remain unaware they have moved, as the IP layer shields movement from upper layer. In cases where these applications have roamed into foreign networks and attempt to initiate unicast or multicast communication using UDP, source address selection procedures stipulate the home address be used by default [1]. To avoid suboptimal routing, it would be beneficial to notify applications to enable them to be movement aware, so that their care-of-addresses can instead be used. This would also be especially useful to applications that are location- and context-sensitive which require rediscovery of essential services for proper operation, such as finding or using a multicast DNS server [2], printing and file services as well as proxy settings.

When multicast-aware applications and devices roam into new networks, they would first need to detect movement into the new network space and subsequently rejoin multicast groups they were previously members of. This reduces latency and the perceived interruption in service, by not waiting for Multicast Listener Queries from the local router in the foreign network before responding and rejoining the multicast groups. Examples are multicast audio/video streaming receivers and agents using multicast-based service discovery protocols such as SLP [3].

Overlay networks such as application-level P2P networks build a routing topology, the performance of which is dependent on efficient connectivity paths among nodes in the underlying network layer. Some overlay or P2P networks are also self-organising and location-aware [4], taking into account changes by nodes entering or leaving the network. Optimal routing decisions in these networks can be achieved if movement information is available to reflect the changing network paths between nodes.

3 Mobinfo: Motivation and Design

Work on Mobinfo draws upon lessons learnt in previously designing a Mobile IPv6 movement detection library specifically for Linux 2.4-based systems, which hooked directly into the kernel source code [5]. For applications, the IETF mip6 (Mobility for IPv6) working group also standardised API support that allows Mobile IPv6 applications and implementations access to Mobility binding messages and Return Routability messages [6], thereby extending the Advanced Socket API for IPv6 [7]. Research has also been done optimising movement detection in Mobile IPv6 [8].

It can be observed that much of the related work in IPv6 movement detection either pertains directly to Mobile IPv6 such as with [5], [6] and [8], requires applications to execute with root privileges such as with [6], or inflexibly supports only a very specific architecture, such as with [5]. In contrast, our aim is for the design of Mobinfo to be more resilient, portable not just across different series of Linux kernels, but also across a range of UNIX and Windows operating systems. It should also provide both movement and interface information independent of whether Mobile IPv6, native fixed IPv6 or transitional IPv6 (such as 6to4 or Teredo) is being used by the terminal. Function calls should be provided for both synchronous (blocking) and asynchronous (non-blocking) modes, to applications needing movement notification. Additionally, Mobinfo should not impose any design or execution constraints onto applications interested in receiving movement information, such as requiring them application to be multithreaded or to execute with root privileges.

Mobinfo is written in ANSI C++. It has been developed and tested using Linux-based nodes. These nodes, apart from having native IPv4 and IPv6 functionality, also support Mobile IPv6 via MIPL [9].

The notification system comprises two components. Firstly it has a shared library which any user program requiring interface information or movement detection is linked against. Secondly it also has a service daemon called Mobinfod which is responsible for obtaining low level information from the interfaces of the device and passing it on to the library. In order to access and examine low-level information, Mobinfod uses a third party packet capture library called libpcap [10]. The daemon and the shared library execute in separate processes; the daemon, together with libpcap runs in one process with privileged permissions, while the shared library, together with the associated application executes in a normal user process. Consequently, FIFO queues are used between the two parts, as FIFOs provide a fairly good implementation for loosely decoupled interprocess communication.

There is a well-known inbound queue for the daemon part which all library instances use in sending their subscription requests. Every library instance also creates an individual queue for receiving messages from the daemon. If necessary, the library instance spawns a thread to handle all non-blocking instances. Should a thread be spawned, it will also receive messages from the daemon via its own FIFO.

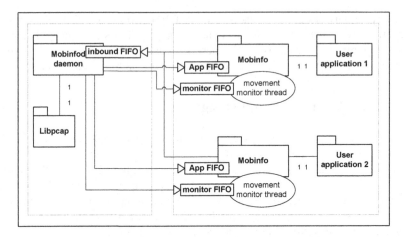

Fig. 1. Architecture of Mobinfo

The overall design and architecture of the movement notification mechanism in UML is depicted by Figure 1, while the facilities of the 2 components are described in greater detail in the following subsections.

3.1 Mobinfo Shared Library Component

The library provides several structures and member functions to applications, to best represent or select the different types of information they need. The following code describes the datatypes defined by the library that applications can use:

```
struct MobinfoAddrInfo {
    short type;
    PrefixType prefix;
    union {
        sockaddr_in ip4_addr;
        sockaddr_in6 ip6_addr;
    } ip_addr;
};

struct MobinfoIface {
    std::string name;
    std::vector< MobinfoAddrInfo > addresses;
};

enum PrefixType {UNKNOWN, UNSPECIFIED, LOOPBACK,
GLOBAL_UNICAST, UNIQUE_LOCAL_UNICAST,LINK_LOCAL_UNICAST,
MULTICAST, _6TO4, TEREDO};
```

The *MobinfoAddrInfo* structure encapsulates IP address information obtained from the daemon to be passed to the application. It currently contains a discriminator to distinguish between an IPv4 or IPv6 address. In addition it contains an enumerated value categorising common address types.

The *MobinfoIface* structure encapsulates the device's interface information. Each structure contains the name of the interface as well as a vector of all addresses associated with the interface.

In addition, the library provides function calls to applications. These function calls (and their signatures in C++) are listed below:

1. bool Mobinfo::getInterfaces(std::vector< std::string >& interfaces)
2. bool Mobinfo::getInterfaceInfo(std::string interface,
                                                      std::vector< MobinfoAddrInfo >& addresses)
3. bool Mobinfo::getAllAddresses(bool ipv4Included, bool ipv6Included,
                                                      std::vector< MobinfoAddrInfo >& addresses)
4. bool Mobinfo::getAllInfo(std::vector< MobinfoIface& info)
5. bool Mobinfo::notifyMovement(void (*callback)(MobinfoIface newinfo))
6. bool Mobinfo::notifyMovement(std::string interface,
                                                      void (*callback)(MobinfoAddrInfo newAddr))
7. void Mobinfo::cancelNotification( )
8. bool Mobinfo::waitForMovement(unsigned int timeout, MobinfoIface& newInfo)
9. bool Mobinfo::waitForMovement(unsigned int timeout, std::string interface,
                                                      MobinfoAddrInfo& newAddr)
10. void Mobinfo::setTimeout(unsigned int timeout)
11. unsigned int Mobinfo::getTimeout( )

Function calls with a *boolean* return value indicate if the requested operation was successfully carried out or not. With the exception of *notifyMovement*, all others are blocking function calls.

GetInterfaces takes a *vector* container of *string* types as a reference and populates the vector container with the names of all known interfaces of the device. *GetInterfaceInfo* accepts one *std::string* parameter representing a specific interface name, searches for an interface with the given name and provides all the addresses attached to that interface into the supplied vector. *GetAllAddresses* can be used if the caller just wants every address available, regardless of the interface. There are two *boolean* parameters that indicate which protocols the caller is interested in: IPv4 and IPv6. Lastly, *getAllInfo* supplies all addresses to the invoking application, categorized by interface.

The *notifyMovement* function calls are non-blocking function calls. The first form simply accepts a callback function as a parameter for invocation whenever any change is detected in any of the device's interfaces. The second form monitors a specific interface, and invokes the callback to return the address information pertaining only to a single interface. Registered callbacks are discarded with the *cancelNotification* function call. The *waitForMovement* function calls are the blocking counterparts to *notifyMovement*. In order to prevent them from blocking indefinitely, a timeout value can be specified in milliseconds. A value of 0 indicates the call should block until movement has occurred.

The *setTimeout* and *getTimeout* functions are used in manipulating timeout values used for communicating by the library with the daemon over the library's FIFO queue with the *poll()* system call. It is given in milliseconds.

3.2 Mobinfo Daemon

Upon startup the daemon queries for all known interfaces and addresses via the low-level API provided by libpcap and stores returned results in its cache. Periodic queries are then issued and results compared with those in the cache. In the case of a new address appearing, movement notification is sent to library instances registered to receive it. The communication between these parts is carried out by using the following sets of messages:

- SUBSCRIBE, SUBSCRIBED_ACK
- UNSUBSCRIBE, UNSUBSCRIBED_ACK
- REQUEST_INFO, NODE_INFO
- REQUEST_MOVEMENT_NOTIFICATION, MOVEMENT_NOTIFICATION
- CANCEL_MOVEMENT_NOTIFICATION, MOVEMENT_NOTIFICATION_CANCELLED_ACK
- UPDATE_QUERY, QUERY_RESPONSE

The SUBSCRIBE and SUBSCRIBED_ACK are only used when a library instance starts communicating with the daemon. Similarly the UNSUBSCRIBE and UNSUBSCRIBED_ACK are used when a library instance wants to end the interaction with the daemon.

A REQUEST_INFO message is used when a library instance wants to update its local information and requests it from the daemon. The daemon then responds with a NODE_INFO which breaks into following sub-messages:

- DATA_HEADER
- DATA
- END_OF_DATA

A DATA_HEADER will always precede a DATA message informing the receiver of which type the DATA is. The receiver can then resolve the DATA message length which is necessary when receiving messages from a FIFO queue. An END_OF DATA message informs the receiver there is nothing further to send.

A REQUEST_MOVEMENT_NOTIFICATION will register the caller to receive movement notifications. The daemon will presume a monitor thread is already running with its own FIFO in the client side and shall send it a MOVEMENT_NOTIFICATION message in the event of movement occurring.

If the library instance is willing to cancel the movement notification it will send a CANCEL_MOVEMENT_NOTIFICATION message to the daemon. The library may not close its inbound queue before the cancelling has been acknowledged by the daemon by using a MOVEMENT_NOTIFICATION_CANCELLED_ACK message.

UPDATE_QUERY message is used by the library when it needs to check if the local address information has been outdated. The daemon will respond to this query with a QUERY_RESPONSE message. Figure 2 shows an example message flow.

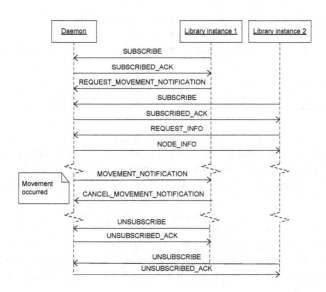

Fig. 2. Interaction between the daemon and library instances

4 Future Work

Although our primary area of interest is developing support for IPv6 (both native and transition-based) and Mobile IPv6 application development, movement notification in IPv4 space can also be easily performed. No support has yet been added to detect moving between public IP addresses and private IP addresses. Additionally, if two distinct networks both use private IPv4 addresses with the same range, difficulties detecting movement would arise when the device moves from one network to another.

Mobinfo uses libpcap to obtain interface and address information. This brings a huge advantage in that libpcap is in constant development to support new protocols, address families and interfaces, both physical and virtual (such as tunnels). Apart from supporting the monitoring of interface addresses in the Internet address families, we can also harness libpcap's experimental abilities in future to obtain information from some Bluetooth protocol stacks to extract movement from local area networks into personal area networks. In addition, we can easily substitute libpcap for winpcap (the Windows equivalent) to allow the execution of Mobinfo in Windows and Windows Mobile platforms, apart from Linux, BSD-based and Mac OS X platforms.

Apart from the function calls now provided to the applications to discover changes to interface addresses, intelligence can be incorporated to also supply more information such as the routability of a newly obtained address. A possible way of accomplishing this would be to utilize libpcap's packet capturing functionality in listening to router advertisements. However at times, this may not be as straightforward. With Mobile IPv6, a new care-of address is obtained whenever a mobile node moves into a new network. Until route optimization procedures are conducted successfully however, the home address would still be the preferred source address with packets using a bidirectional tunnel to the mobile node's home agent.

Other forms of movement detection can also be added into the notification system. An interesting development that needs to be considered is movement in geographic spaces. This could be accomplished if the mobile device possesses GPS reception capabilities.

5 Conclusion

Innovative, adaptive and context-aware applications today are poised to take advantage of their immediate surroundings for interaction, both with the user as well as with other surrounding devices. Often, the need for obtaining movement detection information is placed at a premium. However, very little work actually exists in bringing this information to such applications in a uniform way.

Mobinfo aims to bridge the gap between lower level interfaces of the device and the application by providing a comprehensive library API that preserves the richness of the information obtained for processing by applications, without application developers needing to devote time to create their own mechanisms. In doing so, it can accelerate the development, deployment time and adoption of a new generation of mobile applications.

References

1. Draves, R.: Default Address Selection for Internet Protocol version 6, RFC 3584 (February 2003)
2. Chesire, S., Krochmal, M.: Multicast DNS, IETF work in progress (August 2006)
3. Guttman, E.: Service Location Protocol Modifications for IPv6, RFC 3111 (May 2001)
4. Wu, C., Liu, D., Hwang, R.: A location-aware peer-to-peer overlay network. International Journal of Communications Systems 20(1), 83–102 (2007)
5. Borst, M., Silverajan, B.: Movement Notification in Mobile IPv6. In: Proceedings of 10th European Summer School and IFIP WG 6.3 Workshop, Tampere, Finland (June 14-16, 2004)
6. Chakrabarti, S., Nordmark, E.: Extension to Sockets API for Mobile IPv6. RFC 4584 (July 2006)
7. Stevens, W., Thomas, M., Nordmark, E., Jinmei, T.: Advanced Sockets Application Program Interface (API) for IPv6. RFC 3542 (May 2003)
8. Daley, G., Pentland, B., Nelson, R.: Movement detection optimizations in Mobile IPv6. In: Proceedings of 11th IEEE International Conference on Networks (ICON 2003), Sydney, Australia, September 28 - October 1, 2003, IEEE Computer Society Press, Los Alamitos (2003)
9. MIPL: MIPL Mobile IPv6 for Linux, http://www.mobile-ipv6.org
10. Libpcap packet capture library, http://www.tcpdump.org

Towards a Rule-Based Approach for Context-Aware Applications*

Laura Daniele, Patrícia Dockhorn Costa, and Luís Ferreira Pires

Centre for Telematics and Information Technology,
University of Twente, Enschede, The Netherlands
{l.m.daniele, p.dockhorncosta, l.ferreirapires}@ewi.utwente.nl

Abstract. Context-aware applications can sense and explore the users' context in order to provide proper and useful services to these users. These applications can react intelligently upon changes in the user's context, performing actions relevant to the user, the application itself, and the interaction between user and application. Context-aware reactive behaviors can be expressed by using rules written in a Domain-specific Language, coined ECA-DL, specially developed for context-aware applications. This paper proposes support for the development of a generic component capable of executing rules written using ECA-DL. This component executes these rules by using Jess, which is a well-known tool for developing rule-based systems.

Keywords: Context-awareness, ECA pattern, ECA-DL, Rule-based systems.

1 Introduction

Context-awareness is a computing paradigm in which applications can determine their behavior by sensing and exploring the users' context without explicit user intervention. These applications can react intelligently upon changes in the user's context by performing actions relevant to the user, the application itself, and the interaction between user and application. We can express this by using a language specially developed for context-aware applications, coined Event-Control-Action Domain-specific Language (ECA-DL) [13].

This paper proposes support for the development of a rule engine component capable of processing context-aware applications behaviors expressed in ECA-DL. This component can be implemented by using Jess, a well-known tool for developing rule-based systems. However, since the Jess rule engine reasons in terms of a specific language, we have to map ECA-DL statements onto the Jess language in order to have these statements being executed. The ultimate goal of this work is to show how this mapping can take place.

The structure of the paper is the following: Section 2 describes context-aware applications and the Event-Control-Action (ECA) pattern, which is an architectural

---

* This work is part of the projects Freeband AWARENESS and A-MUSE (http://awareness. freeband.nl, http://a-muse.freeband.nl). Freeband is sponsored by the Dutch government under contract BSIK 03025.

A. Pras and M. van Sinderen (Eds.): EUNICE 2007, LNCS 4606, pp. 33–43, 2007.

pattern that facilitates the development of context-aware applications, Section 3 presents the ECA-DL language, Section 4 describes the Jess architecture, Section 5 discusses the mapping from ECA-DL onto Jess by means of a case study, Section 6 discusses some related work on context-aware applications based on ECA rules, and Section 7 presents our conclusions and identifies topics for future work.

2   Context-Awareness

In the area of ubiquitous and pervasive computing, context is considered as key in the efforts to disperse and enmesh computation into people's lives. Context-aware applications aim to acquire and utilize information about the context of a device and its user to provide services that are appropriate to particular people, place, time and events [1].

Context-awareness implies intelligence that enables an application to discover, reason and predict a situation, and adapt to it in a dynamically changing environment. Applications operating in distributed environments also had to become mobile, in particular when servicing people on the move. In order to produce real awareness in ubiquitous and pervasive computing, programs with embedded intelligence also had to become mobile and retrieve context-related information in different locations. Thus, mobility aids in the intelligent acquisition of context [2].

2.1   Context-Aware Applications

In our work we start from the definition of context given in [3], which is: *"Context is a collection of interrelated circumstances in which something exists or occurs"*.

In the development of context-aware applications we have to cope with context discovery, sensing, extraction, manipulation and interpretation. Actually, we need to create a correspondence between objects in the real world and objects in the applications, since circumstances sensed by the environment in real world cannot be directly used by the applications. Therefore, it is necessary to represent these *circumstances* for the real world, which form the context, in terms of *context information*, characterized by specific values, which we call *context conditions*.

Fig. 1 shows the context of a person (application user) in real world and context-aware applications that can only refer to this context through context information [4].

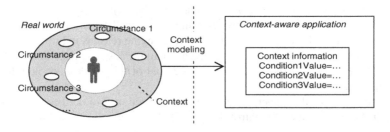

Fig. 1. Context in real world versus context information in context-aware applications

We can define many different kinds of context circumstances. For example, the geographical location in which the user can be found, environmental circumstances of the physical environment of the user, such as temperature, humidity, light, etc., or the user's vital signs like the heart beat or the blood pressure.

2.2   Event-Control-Action (ECA) Pattern

Whenever some specific circumstances change in the user's context, the applications should be able to consequently adjust their behavior. For this purpose we can use the Event-Control-Action (ECA) pattern [5]. The Event-Control-Action (ECA) pattern is an architectural pattern that can facilitate the development of context-aware applications, since it presents solutions for recurring problems associated with managing context information and reacting upon context changes.

Fig. 2 shows that the ECA pattern divides the tasks of gathering and processing context information (*Event* module), from tasks of triggering actions in response to context changes (*Action* module). These separate tasks are realized under the control of an application behavior description (*Control* module), in which reactive context-aware application behaviors are described in terms of ECA rules, also called *condition rules*. These rules have the form *if<condition> then <action>*. The condition part of an ECA rule specifies the situation under which the actions are enabled, and it consists of logical combinations of *events*. An event models some happening of interest in our application or its environment. The action part of the rule consists of one or more actions that are triggered whenever the condition part is satisfied [5].

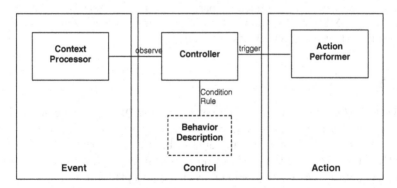

Fig. 2. Event-Control-Action pattern in context-aware applications

Therefore, the ECA pattern reflects the reactive nature of context-aware applications, whose behaviors can be expressed in ECA rules. In order to allow ECA rules to be expressed and manipulated, we have developed a language to define them. This language has been developed in the scope of the Freeband AWARENESS project [6] and is coined ECA Domain-specific Language (ECA-DL).

3 ECA-DL

ECA-DL is a *Domain-specific Language* specially targeted to context-aware applications. Rules in ECA-DL consist of an *Event* part that models an occurrence of interest in the context, a *Condition* part that specifies a condition that must hold prior to the execution of the action, and an *Action* part to be executed when conditions are fulfilled. Often the Action part of a rule consists of the invocation of a notification service, but it could also be any operation needed by the application. ECA-DL rules follow the ECA pattern, and, therefore, they can be used for specifying ECA rules.

ECA-DL has been developed with the following requirements in mind [14]:

- *Expressive power*, in order to enable the specification of complex event relations. ECA-DL allows the use of relational operator predicates (e.g., <, >, =) and the use of logical connectives (e.g., AND, OR, NOT) on events, allowing compound conditions to be built;
- *Convenient use*, in order to facilitate its utilization by context-aware application developers. ECA-DL provides high-level constructs that facilitate the definition of event compositions;
- *Extensibility*, in order to allow extension of predicates to accommodate events being defined on demand, as well as event properties.

In ECA-DL, context changes are described as changes in situation states. *Situations* represent specific instances of context information, typically high level context information. Situations may be defined upon other situations or facts. *Facts* define current "state of affairs" in the user's environment.

Facts and situations are defined as part of information models, which we have defined using UML class diagrams. Our models define entities, context, and mutual relationships between each entity and its context.

4 Jess

In order to find a suitable technology to execute ECA-DL rules, we compared some available tools for developing rule-based system, namely CLIPS [7], Jess [8], jDREW [10] and Mandarax [11], and Jess appeared to be the most appropriate choice. Jess (Java Expert System Shell) is a fast and powerful rule engine that supports the development of rule-based systems and runs on the Java platform.

A rule-based system basically consists of *facts* and *rules*. Facts represent all the pieces of information the rules work with. The general form of a Jess rule is:

```
(defrule RuleName "comment"
(fact_1). . . (fact_N) => (action_1) . . . (action_M))
```

Jess rules have two parts: a left hand side (LHS) and right hand side (RHS). The LHS is strictly defined for matching fact patterns. The RHS defines a list of actions to be performed if the pattern(s) of the LHS is (are) satisfied. Actions are typically method calls. Fig. 3 shows the Jess architecture.

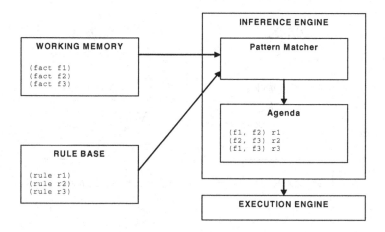

Fig. 3. The Jess architecture

The *working memory* contains facts, which can be used as both LHS and RHS of the rules. The Jess working memory is similar to a relational database: facts are like rows of a database, with indexes to speed up searching in the working memory. The *rule base* contains all the rules the engine knows. The *inference engine* decides what rules to fire and when, and consists of the *pattern matcher* and the *agenda*.

The *pattern matcher* decides which rules to activate based on the contents of the working memory. A rule is activated when the pattern matcher finds facts that satisfy the LHS of this rule, assuming a forward chaining reasoning. The *agenda* stores the list of rules that could be potentially fired. The agenda consists of an ordered list of rules, whose RHS can be executed. The agenda has to decide which rules have the highest priority and should be fired first. This process is called *conflict resolution strategy* and usually it takes into account the specificity or complexity of each rule, and the relative age of the LHS of each rule in the working memory.

Finally, the *execution engine* fires the rules, by executing the RHS of each rule that the inference engine has decided to fire [9].

5   Mapping ECA-DL to Jess

Jess can only process rules expressed in the Jess language. Therefore, since we want to use Jess to execute ECA-DL rules, we need to define mappings from ECA-DL onto the Jess language. We have performed some case studies in order to identify these mappings. Based on our experience with these cases studies, we defined guidelines for these mappings, which can be used as input for automated translation.

5.1   General Approach

Fig. 4 shows the general approach we have taken for designing the mappings.

An information model in ECA-DL consists of a UML class diagram that depicts entities and contexts, reflecting the knowledge that the target context-aware

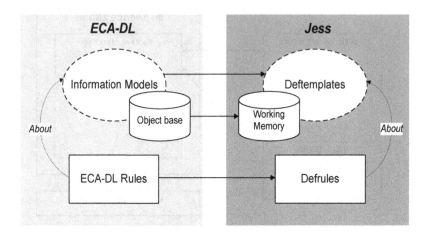

Fig. 4. Design of the mapping from ECA-DL onto Jess: general approach

application manipulates. Entities and context are represented as classes, and the relationships between them are defined as associations between these classes. A `deftemplate` in Jess is the static structure to define the structure of facts. We need to define `deftemplates` before asserting any facts in the working memory of the rule engine. The first step in our approach has been to provide a mapping from the ECA-DL information models to `deftemplates` in Jess.

We can create instances of the classes represented in an ECA-DL information model. These instances are the objects contained in the object base shown in Fig. 4. Analogously to defining objects in ECA-DL, we can also assert facts with specific values in Jess. These facts reflect the structure of the `deftemplates` and they are contained in the working memory of the Jess engine. Therefore, the operation to create objects in ECA-DL corresponds to the operation to assert facts in Jess. The second step in our approach has been to provide a mapping from one or more ECA-DL objects in the object base to facts in the working memory of Jess.

Fig. 4 shows that ECA-DL rules are based on information models. Analogously, Jess rules, defined with the `defrule` command, are based on `deftemplates`. ECA-DL rules use objects that are instances of the entity and context classes of the information model. Likewise, `defrule` constructs in Jess use facts asserted on previously defined `deftemplates`. The third and last step in our approach has been to provide a mapping from ECA-DL rules to `defrules` by investigating the correspondences between ECA-DL specific constructs to Jess constructs.

5.2 Case Study

Consider the following scenario:

"During the hot season, when the temperature in a building of the University of Twente is more than 30 degrees and it is later than 14:00 hours and earlier than 17:00 hours, all the persons in the building should be notified to go home".

We have expressed this scenario by using the following ECA rule:

If <During the hot season the temperature in a building of the University of Twente is more than 30 degrees AND it is later than 14:00 hours AND it is earlier than 17:00 hours > *then* <Notify (all the persons in the building), "You can go home.">

Fig. 5 represents the mapping from the ECA-DL information model corresponding to this rule onto `deftemplates` in Jess.

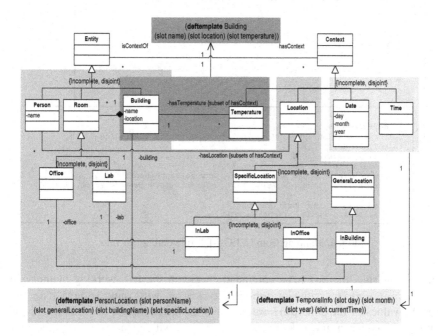

Fig. 5. General mapping from an ECA-DL information model to Jess `deftemplates`

In Fig. 5, the association hasLocation between the entity Person and the context Location has been mapped onto a PersonLocation `deftemplate`. The association hasTemperature between the entity Building and the context Temperature has been mapped onto a `deftemplate` called Building. A Building has a name (slot name in the template), a location (slot location), which in our case is the University of Twente, and a temperature (slot temperature). The context Date and Time have been mapped onto a `deftemplate` called TemporalInfo. Date has attributes day, month, year that are mapped, respectively, onto the slots day, month, year of the `deftemplate`, while Time has been mapped onto the slot currentTime.

Fig. 6 presents the ECA-DL rule we have used to describe the desired application behavior, and the Jess rule onto which this ECA-DL rule has been mapped. In the ECA-DL rule, the **Select**(building.*, build, build.inUT) clause defines all building located in the University of Twente and the **Scope** clause stores this set of buildings in a variable b. The rule is executed upon the event EnterTrue (b.temperature>30), i.e., when the temperature in a building of the University of Twente is more than 30 degrees, and when the additional conditions currentTime >

14 and `currentTime` < `17` are fulfilled. The **Do** clause selects all the persons in a building b, i.e., in the building of the University of Twente where the temperature is more than 30 degrees, in order to notify them to go home. Finally, since the rule should be executed during the hot season, the lifetime associated with the rule is **from** `<May>` **to** `<September>`, which are the hottest months of the year.

```
                                ECA-DL

   Scope (Select (building.*, build, build.inUT); b)
   Upon EnterTrue (b.temperature > 30)
   When currentTime > 14) AND (currentTime < 17)
   Do    Notify (Select (person.*, p, p.inBuilding(b)),
   "You can go home")
   from <May> to <September>
```

```
                                 Jess
   (defrule example2
   (PersonLocation (personName ?p)(generalLocation inBuilding)
   (buildingName ?b1))
   (Building (name ?b2&:(eq ?b2 ?b1))(location inUT)
   (temperature    ?temp&:(> ?temp 30)))
   (TemporalInfo (month May|June|July|August|September)
   (currentTime ?time&:(> ?time 14)) (currentTime ?time&:(< ?time 17)))
   =>
   (bind ?class (New Notification))
   (call ?class SendNotification ?p))
```

Fig. 6. Mapping from an ECA-DL rule onto a Jess rule

In the Jess rule, the **defrule** command checks in the Jess working memory for facts `PersonLocation` with slot `generalLocation` with value `inBuilding`, and stores the values of the slots `personName` and `buildingName`, in variables `?p` and `?b`, respectively. Then, it checks for facts `Building` with a slot `name` with the same value of the slot `buildingName`, a slot `location` with value `inUT`, and a slot `temperature` with a value higher than 30 degrees. Finally, it checks for a fact `TemporalInfo` with a slot `months` with value `May` or `June` or `July` or `August` or `September`, and a slot `currentTime` with a value between 14 and 17.

If the engine finds all these facts, it executes the RHS of the rule, which creates an object named `?class` by instantiating the `Notification` class and calls a method `SendNotification` on this object in order to notify `?p` (i.e., all the persons that have location in a building of the UT with a temperature higher than 30 degrees).

The clauses **Scope** (**Select** `(building.*, build, build.inUT); b)`) and **Upon** EnterTrue `(b.temperature > 30)` have been mapped onto the slots `(location inUT)` and `(temperature ?temp&:(> ?temp 30))` of the fact `Building` in the LHS of the **defrule**.

The **When** clause has been mapped onto the slots `(currentTime ?time&:(> ?time 14))` and `(currentTime ?time&:(< ?time 17))` of the fact `TemporalInfo` in the LHS.

The **Do** clause has been mapped onto the RHS of the **defrule**, but the clause **Select** `(person.*, p, p.InBuilding(b))` corresponds to the following code in the LHS:

```
(PersonLocation(personName ?p)(generalLocation inBuilding)
(buildingName ?b1))
(Building (name ?b2&:(eq ?b2 ?b1))
(location inUT)(temperature ?temp&:(> ?temp 30)))
```

Finally, the lifetime **from** <May> **to** <September> has been mapped onto the slot (month May|June|July|August|September) of the fact TemporalInfo in the LHS.

6 Related Work

Although considerable efforts have been made in rule-based context-aware applications to map ECA rules to a language of choice, none of the efforts we found in the literature use Jess as software environment to support the mapping.

In [15], a CORBA-based ECA Rule Matching Service is presented. This service complements the Standard CORBA Notification Service with a Composite Event Matching Engine based on CLIPS. This service highly simplifies the development of reactive applications by alleviating the programmer from the implementation of complex composite event handling mechanism. Although CLIPS provides a proper rule-based environment to execute ECA rules, Jess is a better choice for our purpose as we have discussed in [12]. Basically, Jess is the Java evolution of CLIPS, which is written in C. Both engines support a high level of extensibility and integration with code written in other programming languages. An important requirement for our work has been to be able to extend the rule engine's standard functionality by using Java, in order to process ECA rules expressed in the ECA-DL language, and Jess fulfils this requirement. Moreover, although both engines provide interactive development environments, Jess comes with JessDE, which is an Eclipse-based development environment that allows the developer to increase productivity. Finally, concerning the language used by these systems and its ease of use, CLIPS language is considered as inconvenient for the programmer because the overuse of parenthesis and the need to use inverse polish notation for building arithmetic and conditional expressions.

In [16], the modeling of complex ad-hoc context-aware scenarios is discussed. These scenarios are defined in terms of a set of ECA rules for each entity that is relevant for the scenario. Towards this aim, a very flexible and stable context middleware software framework was implemented and tested for an example scenario. Nevertheless, the drawback of this framework is that it cannot guarantee the consistency of rules by reasoning about entities and their relationships. In the reported implementation, the task to trigger actions according to incoming events is performed by an interpreter component within the framework, which is not able to check the consistency of new rules. Therefore, in order to manage entity relationship reasoning, the authors plan to integrate the Jess library into the context framework that they have realized. In our work, we considered that the usage of an available expert system shell like Jess reduces the cost and time of development compared with writing the expert system from scratch, as it has been done in [16].

7 Conclusions and Future Work

In [12] we have reported on the mapping of ECA-DL rules onto the Jess language and, based on case studies similar to the one above, we have been able to identify patterns and generalize these mappings. More detail on the case studies and mapping guidelines can be found in [12].

Future work consists of the improvement, generalization and automation of the mapping in order to enhance productivity and provide an automatic translation of ECA-DL rules (i.e., of the Upon, When, Do, Select, Scope clauses) to Jess defrules. Currently, work is being done to specify and implement this automatic translation as a transformation based on the metamodels of the ECA-DL and the Jess languages. This way, changes in the ECA-DL specifications can automatically reflect to the deftemplates structures in Jess.

In addition, it would be interesting to provide a mapping from ECA-DL to a generic rule engine model, which is not specific to any particular technology. This generic model could be mapped onto different engines, such as the ones that we have studied in [12], with little effort. In this way the mapping effort concentrates on creating a generic model of an application that can be mapped straightforwardly to specific technologies.

References

1. Moran, T.P., Dourish, P.: Introduction to This Special Issue on Context-Aware Computing. Human Computer Interaction 16, 87–95 (2001)
2. Zaslavsky, A.: Mobile Agents: Can They Assist with Context Awareness? In: MDM'04. IEEE International Conference on Mobile Data Management, p. 304. IEEE Computer Society Press, Los Alamitos (2004)
3. Context: Merriam-Webster Online Dictionary page. Available at [http://www.m-w.com/dictionary/context]
4. Dockhorn Costa, P., Ferreira Pires, L., van Sinderen, M.: Architectural Support for Mobile Context-Aware Applications. In: Handbook of Research on Mobile Multimedia, pp. 456–475. Idea Group Inc. (2006)
5. Dockhorn Costa, P., Ferreira Pires, L., van Sinderen, M.: Architectural Patterns for Context-Aware Services Platform. In: Proceedings of the Second International Workshop on Ubiquitous Computing (IWUC 2005), Miami (May 2005)
6. Freeband AWARENESS project. Available at [http://awareness.freeband.nl]
7. CLIPS website. Available at [http://www.ghg.net/clips/CLIPS.html]
8. Jess website. Available at [http://herzberg.ca.sandia.gov/jess/]
9. Friedman-Hill, E.: Jess in Action: Java Rule Based Systems. Manning Publications Co. (2003)
10. jDREW website. Available at [http://www.jdrew.org/jDREWebsite/jDREW.html]
11. Mandarax website. Available at [http://mandarax.sourceforge.net/]
12. Daniele, L.M.: Towards a Rule-Based Approach for Context-Aware Applications. Thesis for a Master of Science Degree in Electronic Engineering from the University of Cagliari, Italy (May 2006), Available at [http://asna.ewi.utwente.nl/education/Student%20assignments/completed%20bachelor%20and%20master%20assignments/daniele.html]

13. Dockhorn Costa, P., Ferreira Pires, L., van Sinderen, M., Broens, T.: Controlling Services in a Mobile Context-Aware Infrastructure. In: CAPS 2006. Proceedings of the Second Workshop on Context Awareness for Proactive Systems, Kassel, Germany (June 2006)
14. Etter, R., Dockhorn Costa, P., Broens, T.: A Rule-Based Approach Towards Context-Aware User Notification Services. In: Proceedings of the IEEE International Conference on Pervasive Services, Lyon, France, June 2006, pp. 281–284. IEEE Computer Society Press, Los Alamitos (2006)
15. de Ipiña, D.L.: An ECA Rule-Matching Service for Simpler Development of Reactive Applications. In: Proceedings of Middleware 2001 at IEEE Distributed Systems Online 2(7) (November 2001)
16. Beer, W., Christian, V., Ferscha, A., Mehrmann, L.: Modeling Context-Aware Behavior by Interpreted ECA Rules. In: Kosch, H., Böszörményi, L., Hellwagner, H. (eds.) Euro-Par 2003. LNCS, vol. 2790, pp. 1064–1073. Springer, Heidelberg (2003)

Semantic Context Reasoning Using Ontology Based Models

Rodrigo Mantovaneli Pessoa[1], Camilo Zardo Calvi[2], José Gonçalves Pereira Filho[2], Cléver Ricardo Guareis de Farias[3], and Ricardo Neisse[1,*]

[1] University of Twente, Enschede – The Netherlands
[2] Federal University of Espírito Santo, Vitória – Brazil
[3] University of São Paulo, Ribeirão Preto – Brazil
{mantovanelir, r.neisse}@ewi.utwente.nl,
{camilozc, zegonc}@inf.ufes.br,
farias@ffclrp.usp.br

Abstract. New mobile computing technologies and the increasing use of portable devices have pushed the development of the so-called *context-aware applications*. This new class of applications aims at improving human-computer interactions by supporting dynamic adaptations according to context changes. This paper discusses the suitability of using ontologies for modeling context information and presents the design, implementation and applicability of an ontology based context interpreter. The proposed interpreter is responsible for inferring new context information in a context-aware services platform.

Keywords: Context-aware, context modeling, context reasoning, ontologies.

1 Introduction

The new mobile standards and technologies, and the increasing use of portable devices have stimulated the development of a new computing paradigm called Pervasive Computing. In contrast to the more traditional desktop-based computing paradigm, Pervasive Computing is characterized by constant changes in the environment caused by the mobility of its users. In this scenario, a new class of applications called context-aware has raised on increasing interest in the research community. Context-aware applications take into account in their processing not only explicit user supplied information, but also implicit information related to user's physical and computational environment. These applications are programmed to react to and explore the constant changes in user's context within a dynamic domain.

The development of context-aware applications deals with a number of technological challenges and requires the existence of a suitable support infrastructure to facilitate the construction and execution of these applications. Particularly, support is needed to deal with different context information sources and types. In this sense, a number of initiatives related to the development of support platforms have been proposed in the literature, e.g., [6], [5], [4], [9]. This work is part of the Infraware

---

* Supported by CNPq Scholarship – Brazil.

A. Pras and M. van Sinderen (Eds.): EUNICE 2007, LNCS 4606, pp. 44–51, 2007.

Service Platform [12][7] which aims at providing a number of services and suitable architectural support for the development of context-aware applications.

One particular problem that has to be addressed by a context-aware service platform is the definition of a model to describe the contextual domain in which a given application or service is defined. Several context models are available in the literature, such as Key-value pairs models [13], Markup Scheme models [6], Object-oriented models [1], and ontology based models [4][9]. The objective of these models is to provide a high level abstraction of context information in order to store, manage, and process the context. However, most of these models lack a formal representation of its syntax and semantics in order to guarantee the consistency between different representations of context used by applications, context providers and service platforms. Furthermore, the level of abstraction provided by the proposed models and the expressivity of their representation language has a significantly impact on the reasoning process.

This paper discusses the suitability of using ontologies for modeling context information and presents the design, implementation and applicability of an ontology based context interpreter. The proposed interpreter is responsible for reasoning context information in a context-aware services platform. The remaining of this work is structured as follows: section 2 presents ontology-based models; section 3 introduces architectural aspects of our context interpreter; section 4 presents implementation details; section 5 describes a usage scenario; section 6 discusses some related work; finally, section 7 presents our conclusions and future work.

2 Ontology-Based Context Models

As already mentioned, one particular problem that should be addressed by context-aware service platforms is the definition of a model describing the context information and the application domain in which one application is inserted.

Ontology based models provide logic characterization for the interpretation of objects, classes and relationships. The formal notation used by this type of model permits the specification of the domain in an ambiguous way, allowing semantically consistent inferences, and also assuring one shared and reusable representation of the contextual information among context providers, service platforms and applications. This enables the development of systems that are able to derive implicit information through the analysis of information represented explicitly.

The OWL (Ontology Web Language) [2] was chosen to specify our context model as it allows the modification and reuse of concepts definition and relations through a well defined and sufficient expressive semantic. OWL is also the language recommended by W3C for ontology and content representation in the semantic web.

3 Conceptual Architecture of Context Interpreter

Our Context Interpreter is divided into five modules as presented in Figure 1: Query Engine, Event Notifier, Working Memory, Inference Engine, and Knowledge Database. These modules together are able to carry on the context reasoning process.

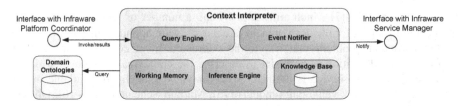

Fig. 1. Conceptual Architecture of Context Interpreter

The five modules share the Domain Ontologies that describe general concepts related to the application domain and their relationships. The storage of the domain ontologies in this repository promotes a shared knowledge organization and allows reuse. Furthermore, the isolation of these specifications permits the extension and redefinition of these ontologies for different domains.

The Knowledge Database stores instantiated knowledge from the Domain Ontologies or, in other words, it represents a specific knowledge representation. This knowledge is specified through a set of if-then rules and known facts. One rule establishes one relationship between clauses (assertions and facts) and, depending on the situation, can be used to generate new information or to fire an action.

The working memory stores known facts and assertions made by the rules. The Inference Engine combines facts from the Working Memory with the Rules Database in order to assert new facts or to identify specific contexts. The Query Engine allows access to the actual state of interpreted facts by the other modules in the Infraware platform. The Event Notifier is responsible for the dispatch of an action from the occurrence of a new event or monitored context.

4   Implementation

In the current implementation, our Context Interpreter uses the Jena Semantic Web Framework API [10] to manipulate and infer contextual information. Jena is a framework based on Java, developed by HP Labs Semantic Web Programme to build applications to support Semantic Web scenarios. Beyond the support of RDF, DAML+OIL and OWL languages, Jena API also offers components to build rule inference engines.

Subscription requests are compiled using inference rules written in GRL (Generic Rule Language), specified by Jena API. These rules express possible contexts and are evaluated by the Context Interpreter, which uses the information sent by context providers to dispatch actions at the occurrence of several events. Using the RDQL (Resource Description Query Language) declarative language [14], the applications can query relevant context information with support to inference and semantic validation.

Figure 2 shows a UML component diagram of the implemented Context Interpreter. The Context Interpreter uses two data files. One file contains OWL domain ontologies (*DomainOntology*) that defines terms to describe and represent an application domain. In this mode, domain ontologies also define a structured vocabulary with possible metadata constraints describing contextual information and related entities. The second file (*DataInstances*) contains instances of the Domain Ontology representing real-world entities and individuals. The process of context interpretation occurs in response to instance data changes, reflecting the real world's state captured by context providers.

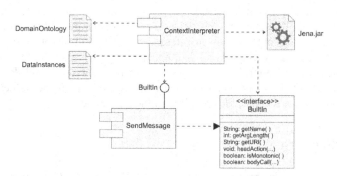

Fig. 2. Context Interpreter Component Diagram

The component *SendMessage* executes a notification service and implements a *BuiltIn* interface. The interface defines a set of methods which implements operators that realize primitive procedure calls. Beyond the operators supplied by Jena API, inference rules can contain personalized operators, like implemented by the *SendMessage* component.

4.1 Inference Engine

The Jena inference system is designed to allow the support of a wide range of inference engines or reasoners. Such engines are used to derive additional assertions which are entailed from some knowledge base together with any ontology information and rules associated with the reasoner. In particular, Jena includes a general purpose rule-based reasoner (Generic Rule Reasoner) which is used to implement both the RDFS and OWL reasoners but is also available for general use.

In our prototype system, we use Jena Generic Rule Reasoner since it supports rule-based inference over RDF graphs and provides forward chaining, backward chaining and a hybrid execution model.

4.2 Generic Rule Language

The Generic Rule Reasoner defines the Generic Rule Language (GRL) to describe inference rules. These rules can derive new facts or dispatch action at the occurrence of specified conditions (events). A rule is defined by a Java *Rule* object with a list of body terms (premises), a list of head terms (conclusions) and an optional name and optional direction. Each term or *ClauseEntry* is a triple pattern, an extended triple pattern or a call to a builtin primitive.

4.3 RDF Data Query Language

Besides the inference of new contextual information and the capability of triggering the dispatch of actions based on event occurrence, the Context Interpreter also allows applications to query for the current state of input and derived context information. These queries are expressed in RDQL [14], a declarative query language for RDF supported by Jena's inference models. RDQL uses a declarative SQL-like syntax for querying information contained in an inference model, often expressed as a set of triples. An RDQL query consists of a graph pattern, expressed as a list of triple patterns. Each triple pattern is comprised of named variables and RDF values. Additionally, a RDQL query can have a set of constraints on the values of those variables, and a list of the variables required in the answer set.

5 Usage Scenario

As a proof of concept in this section we present the use of our Context Interpreter in the development of a tourism application. The implementation of this application has allowed us to evaluate the project decisions related to the modeling and inference of context information as well as to evaluate the technical aspects of the technology used in the implementation of our Context Interpreter component.

Taking as a reference scenario one tourist (user) strolling in an unknown city, applications such as interactive maps, personalized tourist advices about tourist interesting points (following the tourist profile and preferences), and access to infrastructure services like gastronomy, and entertainment (hotels, restaurants, cinemas, theaters, etc.) could be able to help. Users are identified as actors in the system and interact with the applications running in portable mobile devices. Figure 3 illustrates a simplified version of the domain ontology we defined for tourism applications describing the main elements of our application domain.

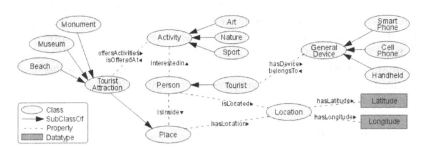

Fig. 3. A simplified tourism domain ontology

One application could be interested in sending users tourist information about a tourist point in the moment the user is in the location. Even though mobile devices allow the access to the information any time and place, it may be interesting to personalize the content of the information sent to users considering the type of the user's device. For example, users of mobile phones with small displays capabilities may fell uncomfortable in reading long messages. Another factor that justifies the personalization of content sent to users is related with the great variation in the resources for presentation of multimedia content in heterogeneous devices. Figure 4 describes two subscription requests (A and B) for tourist information for different classes of devices.

```
[subsc01:(?t rdf:type Tourist)
       (?t hasDevice ?d)
       (?d rdf:type MobilePhone)
       (?t isInside ?p)
       (?p rdf:type TouristAttraction)
 -> SendSMSTouristInformation(?d,?p)]
```

(A)

```
[subsc02:(?t rdf:type Tourist)
       (?t hasDevice ?d)
       (?d rdf:type SmartPhone)
       (?t isInside ?p)
       (?p rdf:type TouristAttraction)
 -> SendMMSTouristInformation(?d,?p)]
```

(B)

Fig. 4. Examples of rules to send tourist information by SMS or MMS messages

The first subscription request (Figure 4–A) calls the information tourist service using SMS messages every time one tourist handling a mobile device of class *MobilePhone* visits one tourist point of interest in the city. The second subscription request (Figure 4–B) send the information to tourists handling devices of the class *SmartPhone* using MMS messages. In both service requests the user device and the point of interest are parameters through the variables "?d" and "?p". Figure 5–A shows how the received messages look like in different types of devices.

(A)   (B)

Fig. 5. Tourist information being received by different types of devices

Another application might be interested in sending users suggestions of places to be visited, according to the users' personal interests. Figure 6 shows an application subscription request using RDQL query in which the tourist points of interest and activities are selected according to the preferences of one specific user. In the example we assume that the user's activities of interest are *Nature* and *Sport*. Figure 5–B shows the result of this query presented to the application user.

```
SELECT ?touristAtraction, ?activity
WHERE (?person, <rdf:type>, <v:Peron>),
      (?person, <v:name>, ?name),
      (?person, <v:InterestedIn>, ?activity),
      (?activity, <v:isOfferedAt>, ?touristAtraction)
   AND ?name eq "Rodrigo Mantovaneli Pessoa"
```

Fig. 6. An example RDQL query retrieving tourist attractions based on user personal interests

6 Related Work

Different approaches for context modeling and reasoning have been proposed in literature. These approaches reflect the diversity of contextual information and its use in different application domains [11].

Schilit et al. [13] propose the use of key-value pairs for the representation of contextual information, which are then used as environment variables. This approach supports only simple value matching comparison, thus limiting its applicability to simple scenarios. Brézillon [3] propose the use of contextual graph for modeling contextual information as nodes in acyclic graphs. New facts about contextual information can be derived by following the graph. Gray and Salber propose a context model that use first order logic to formally represent the transformations and relationships involving contextual information [8].

Ontologies have also been used for context modeling. The Context Broker Architecture (CoBrA) [4] provides an agent-based architecture for the development of context-aware application. Central to this architecture is an intelligent agent called Context Broker that maintains an ontology-based shared model of context on the behalf of a community of agents, services, and devices.

7 Conclusions

This paper proposes the use of a context interpreter to support the development, deployment and execution of context-aware applications. The proposed context interpreter relies on ontology-based semantic descriptions of contextual information to reason and interpret context.

The use of an ontology-based context interpreter allows the definition of formal and extensible models to describe a particular application domain through the specification of a number of concepts, relations and axioms. The extensibility property provided by the use of ontologies allows the introduction of changes in the underlying context model with minimal impact on the applications that depends on this model. Additionally, the specification of the contextual information semantics in a particular application domain allows the interpretation and inference of new contextual information, based on the described contextual model.

Currently, we are working towards the definition of a more generic context ontology using OWL that can be used in different application domains. The existence of such ontology would facilitate the mapping of context information between different context models, thus increasing the degree of portability and interoperability between context-aware applications. Additionally, we will consider the definition of concepts related to the quality and consistency of contextual information.

Acknowledgments

This work has been supported by CNPq under project number 50.6284/2004-2.

This work is part of the Freeband AWARENESS and A-MUSE projects. Freeband is sponsored by the Dutch government under contract BSIK 03025.

References

1. Bardram, J.E.: The Java Context Awareness Framework (JCAF). In: Gellersen, H.-W., Want, R., Schmidt, A. (eds.) PERVASIVE 2005. LNCS, vol. 3468, pp. 98–115. Springer, Heidelberg (2005)
2. Bechhofer, S., van Harmelen, F., et al.: OWL Web Ontology Language Reference: W3C Recommendation (2004), http://www.w3.org/TR/2004/REC-owl-ref-20040210/
3. Brézillon, P.: Context-based modeling of operators' practices by contextual graphs. In: Proceedings of the 14th Conference on Human Centered Processes, pp. 129–137 (2003)
4. Chen, H.: An Intelligent Broker Architecture for Pervasive Context-Aware Systems. Ph.D. Thesis, University of Maryland, USA (2004)
5. Costa, P.D.: Towards a Services Platform for Context-Aware Applications. Master Thesis, University of Twente, Enschede, The Netherlands (2003)
6. Dey, A.K.: Providing Architectural Support for Building Context-Aware Applications. Ph.D. Thesis, Georgia Institute of Technology, USA (2000)
7. Farias, C.R.G., Leite, M.M., Calvi, C.Z., Pessoa, R.M., Pereira Filho, J.G.: A MOF Metamodel for the Development of Context-Aware Mobile Applications. In: Proceedings of the 2007 ACM Symposium on Applied Computing, Seul, pp. 947–952. ACM Press, New York (2007)
8. Gray, P.D., Salber, D.: Modelling and Using Sensed Context Information in the Design of Interactive Applications. In: Nigay, L., Little, M.R. (eds.) EHCI 2001. LNCS, vol. 2254, pp. 317–336. Springer, Heidelberg (2001)
9. Gu, T., Pung, H.K., Zhang, D.Q.: A Service-Oriented Middleware for Building Context-Aware Services. Elsevier Journal of Network and Computer Applications 28(1), 1–18 (2005)
10. McBride, B.: Jena: Implementing the RDF model and syntax specification. In: Proceedings of the 2nd International Workshop on the Semantic Web (2001)
11. Mostéfaoui, G.K., Pasquier-Rocha, J., Brezillon, P.: Context-Aware Computing: A Guide for the Pervasive Computing Community. In: Proceedings of the IEEE/ACS International Conference on Pervasive Services (ICPS´04), pp. 39–48. IEEE Computer Society Press, Los Alamitos (2004)
12. Pereira Filho, J.G., Pessoa, R.M., Calvi, C.Z., et al.: Infraware: Um Middleware de Suporte a Aplicações Móveis Sensíveis ao Contexto (In Portuguese) (Infraware: Middleware Support for Context-Aware Mobile Applications). In: Proceedings of the: 24° 24th Brazilian Symposium on Computer Networks, Curitiba-PR, Brazil (2006)
13. Schilit, W.N., Adams, N.I., Want, R.: Context-Aware Computing Applications. In: Proceedings of the Workshop on Mobile Computing Systems and Applications, pp. 85–90. IEEE Computer Society, Los Alamitos (1994)
14. Seaborne, A.: RDQL - A Query Language for RDF, www.w3.org/Submission/2004/SUBM-RDQL-20040109/

VoIP Codec Adaptation Algorithm in Multirate 802.11 WLANs: Distributed vs. Centralized Performance Comparison

Anna Sfairopoulou, Carlos Macián, and Boris Bellalta

Network Technologies and Strategies (NeTS) Research Group
Universitat Pompeu Fabra
Passeig de Circumval.lació, 8, 08003 Barcelona, Spain
{anna.sfairopoulou, carlos.macian, boris.bellalta}@upf.edu

Abstract. Multirate 802.11 environments are quite problematic for VoIP traffic, with the rate changes of some of the flows affecting the transmission of all others. Building upon our previous results, we propose an algorithm which, based on the combined feedback from Real-Time Control Protocol (RTCP) packets and the MAC layer, can dynamically adapt the codecs of ongoing VoIP calls to adjust them to the multirate scenario. A comparison of both the centralized and distributed versions of the algorithm is provided for a wired-wireless scenario, showing an important capacity and quality increase over the standard case.

1 Introduction

Wireless Voice over IP is becoming increasingly popular as an economic alternative to traditional fixed telephony or even to cellular telephony. Nevertheless, in spite of the equal success and evolution of both VoIP and wireless networks as two separate areas, there are still problems when trying to provide voice services over 802.11 networks. The strict QoS requirements of voice transmission are often unaccomplished due to the specific nature of wireless environments, like unfairness between uplink and downlink streams [6], VoIP degradation in presence of TCP flows [1] or variable capacity due to multi-rate transmissions [2].

Multi-rate transmission is one of the key features of the IEEE 802.11 [3] PHY/MAC specifications which allow each mobile station (STA) to select its physical layer parameters (modulation and channel coding) to optimize the bit transmission over the noise/fading-prone channel. In this environment, sporadic rate changes occur to one or more STA, produced by such effects as increases in distance between the two wireless end-points, presence of walls when entering a room, atmospheric issues (rain, etc.). However, when a STA reduces its rate, the saturation point for the shared channel is reduced, affecting all active calls independently of whether they observe good or bad channel conditions [2]. As a consequence, a rate change produces a general degradation on the performance of the system, with active calls being dropped and reducing the free space for new ones, which result in higher blocking probabilities, provoking an overall

A. Pras and M. van Sinderen (Eds.): EUNICE 2007, LNCS 4606, pp. 52–61, 2007.

suboptimal allocation of the network resources. This effect can be observed in Figure 1, where the feasible distribution of simultaneous VoIP calls in a cell is depicted: considering the use of the *G*.711 voice codec for two types of VoIP calls, the *fast* and the *slow* ones, which use a data rate of 11 Mbps and 1 Mbps respectively, the maximum number of active calls drops as fast calls change to slow calls. For example, with 9 VoIP calls active, if just 1 call changes to the lower rate, the new state becomes not feasible, provoking that all active calls perceive a QoS degradation, as they can not obtain their required bandwidth. Figure 1 has been obtained using the DCF (Distributed Coordination Function) analytical model presented in [1] and adapted for the multi-rate case.

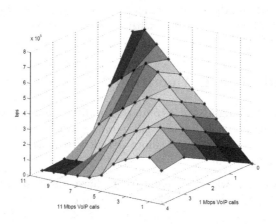

Fig. 1. Bandwidth obtained by the active calls in the presence of fast and slow calls

To the best of our knowledge, there has been few previous work on the problems that multirate wireless LANs introduce to VoIP. Some similar solutions proposing codec adaptation are the ones mentioned here. The authors in [18] focus on the Access Point (AP) acting as a bottleneck problem and propose a centralized element which performs transcoding of incoming calls to the wireless network. The work presented in [17] measures cell congestion and changes the codecs of *all* active calls accordingly, while performing admission control for new calls. Our solution is much lighter in processing effort than transcoding, can be implemented equally in a distributed way since it does not depend on a central server and only *some* of the calls need to adapt their codec. In [9] a similar mechanism to ours is proposed, but there is no consideration of cross-layer information, neither of the specific problem caused by the multirate environment. Another group of related works are the ones focusing on multirate codecs, like AMR (Adaptive MultiRate) in [8] and [14]. AMR was designed mostly for GSM/UMTS networks, where bad channel conditions refer to the ones perceived individually on each STA's channel. In the working scenario studied here, the behavior of other nodes (which change from *fast* to *slow* rates) is what impacts over the system's performance, without any channel change occurring on the fast nodes. Finally, many of the current works focus on changes of the MAC specification, like the one in [7], which proposes a new media access scheme in order to improve the capacity of the wireless cell. However, these solutions require changes on the 802.11 MAC standard while the solution proposed here can be implemented easily without any modifications on the MAC or any other protocol.

This paper proposes a Codec Adaptation Algorithm (CAA), which based on cross-layer information from RTCP and MAC layer can monitor the quality of the active calls and change their codec to adapt them to the multirate environment. Continuing the work already presented in [15][16], the focus here is on a performance evaluation of the different implementations of the CAA; centralized installed on the AP and distributed placed on each STA. Both implementations share the same basic core functions, with small changes between the two that will be explained later.

2   Codec Adaptation Algorithm

The Codec Adaptation algorithm is composed of three main phases: the *monitoring phase*, the *adaptation phase*, and the *recovery phase*, presented below very briefly due to space constraints. A more detailed explanation of the different phases can be found in [16].

Monitoring: Starting with the monitoring phase, the two procedures, MAC and RTCP monitoring, work simultaneously, each one focusing on the problem from a different angle; while MAC monitoring provides a proactive measurement, proposing to take action *before* any quality alarm arrives, RTCP monitoring responds to the alarm signals *after* they happen, in a reactive way. During the MAC monitoring the algorithm reacts on MAC alarms over rate changes. Since just one rate drop can provoke a big impact on all the calls of the cell, the moment that such event is detected the node drops immediately to a one-step lower codec in the codec ranking (codecs are ordered based on their bitrate as seen in chapter 4). This way we obtain a faster reaction to situations that are most probably going to provoke a system degradation and also a more fair solution, since the first to suffer the consequences of the rate change is the node that provoked it. The same procedure works also when there is a rate increase; the node that detects its rate changing to a higher one, changes proactively to a one-step higher rate codec, to fully use its new rate and as a result, obtain better quality on voice transmission.

If the codec change invoked by the MAC layer was not enough to re-stabilize the situation on the cell or if some other cause (like wireless channel errors) is causing additional problems, then this will be detected in the RTCP filtering. The information obtained from the RTCP packets includes critical parameters for voice traffic, such as the number of lost packets and end-to-end delay. These data are used, in order to calculate the R-factor of each flow (a real-time QoS metric proposed by International Telecommunications Union [5]). The equivalence of this factor to the better known Mean Opinion Score (MOS) can define a first QoS decision threshold; if R-factor value falls below 70 (equivalent to MOS 3.6) the quality of the voice flow is not satisfactory and the algorithm triggers the adaptation phase for a new codec selection.

Adaptation: Passing to the adaptation phase, a random timeout is set, during which the node sends a minimum of N fast RTCP packets (with N set to 3 in the simulations) in shorter intervals than the regular ones, in order to collect additional information and make sure that the alarm situation still continues. This timer is also necessary so that not all nodes will react simultaneously, even if all of them perceive the alarm signals at the same instant. This way, the change of codec for more calls than necessary is avoided and the system has some time to recover after every codec change. The interval between the transmission of the "fast RTCP packets" can be set to be lower than the standard 5 seconds interval of RTCP transmission, as defined in the proposal presented in [13] (in our simulation is set to 1 sec). This way the total process delay can be minimized to a few seconds only. We have calculated an estimation of the total overload that these packets would introduce at the network and found that the overhead provoked by the control traffic is very small (around 1.2%) compared with the data traffic of a VoIP call using $G.711$ codec.

When the timer expires the algorithm calculates the average of the R-factor from the information collected during this time and from there the MOS, as also the average of packet loss and delay. CAA compares the average values as well as the current values of the parameters after the timeout against a set of thresholds, chosen using the common values of permitted QoS parameters for an acceptable voice transmission ($delay < 150ms$, packet loss$< 3\%$, $R > 70$). From the result of this comparison and the codec used until now in the transmission, the node can choose a new codec, using the following procedure:

a) if the average value of the parameter is out of the threshold then check its current value; if the current value is also out of threshold propose a codec of α steps lower in the codec ranking, otherwise propose a β steps lower codec.

b) if both the average and the current value of the parameter are above the thresholds then there is no need to change the codec.

This comparison is performed for each one of the three parameters (delay, loss, R) used in the evaluation and from each comparison a codec is proposed. The codec finally chosen is the average of the three proposals. Note that $\alpha > \beta$, with $\alpha = 2$ and $\beta = 1$ in the simulations, and that the codecs are ordered based on their bit rates, as explained in the results section.

Recovery: After the new codec selection, the node is responsible for issuing and sending a re-Invite SIP message to the other end, so as to renegotiate the new call characteristics. If the other end accepts the new codec the call continues normally, otherwise the call is dropped. If the codec proposed as the most appropriate is lower than the lowest codec that a node can support, the call can continue as it is during some stand-by time, without any codec change. If during this time some other node changes codec and the problem is solved then the call can continue successfully, otherwise the call will be dropped. Especially in the centralized version, the AP can choose to change the codec of another call since the present call cannot change any further. Although this way a call drop can be avoided, this extra waiting time would introduce more delay in the recovery process. This part of the algorithm has not yet been tested thoroughly and is part of the ongoing work.

3   Centralized vs. Distributed Architecture

The CAA presented above can be implemented both in a distributed and in a centralized mode with small changes between the two implementations, but with visible difference in performance and results. In the distributed scenario, the algorithm is located on each node and each node monitors its own state. When a rate change is noticed on the MAC layer or based on the RTCP information that is arriving to it, the node is the one to determine whether or not to change codec. This is a more local approach and the node can only decide on the calls depending on it, which may not be the globally optimal solution. As we have proved in our previous work [15], there is no need for all calls to change codec at the same time, and changing slow-rate calls gives better results than changing fast-rate calls. This is due to slow-calls being the ones actually causing the problem, as seen in the problem statement. In the distributed implementation the algorithm cannot give priority to the slow calls, other than the one given by the proactive change, as the call that detects first the QoS drop will be the first to react. Additionally, since the control of the waiting timer is not centralized, more nodes can coincide and change simultaneously codec. Nevertheless, the distributed approach is easy to implement and it distributes the processing load of the algorithm.

In the centralized case, the AP is in charge of monitoring all calls, the transmission rate of each flow and the codec used by each client. When a call passes from fast to slow then the AP, apart from changing the codec of it in a proactive way, can also determine which and how many other calls must change codec so as to reach network stability again, based on the RTCP information exchange between the clients. Intercepting the RTCP packets in their way from one end to the other, it calculates the instantaneous MOS value for all calls. When these values fall below the thresholds, the AP chooses the calls with the worst performance and decides which calls to change and to which codec, giving more weight and priority in changing the slow calls first. Between each codec change, the AP waits during a random time, which permits that less number of calls will have to change. The drawback of this implementation is the amount of processing work for the AP. It must intercept all RTCP packets between the two ends of the voice flows and filter them to obtain the information it needs. When there is a codec change decision, it must inform the node that there is the need to change codec and therefore suggest to issue a SIP re-Invite message to renegotiate the codec with the other end. This can be more complicated than in the distributed version, but on the other hand there is a better overall monitoring of the whole network and there are more possibilities of achieving an optimal codec combination among the nodes. Simulation results show that there is an improvement in the performance of the algorithm when used in its centralized version; We have less calls changing codec, the packet loss percentage is almost zero and the overall MOS achieved is higher than in the distributed implementation. These results will be reviewed in the following section.

4   Simulation Results

The scenario considered is a hot-spot multirate scenario, where the network is composed by one 802.11e [4] basic service set with 9 wireless nodes and one AP connected to the wired network. A total number of 9 calls are active during the simulations, with all of them established between one wired and one wireless client, while the AP is also acting as a Proxy Server. All nodes start by using 11 Mbps data rate (fast-rate calls) and at the instant $t = 95$ of the simulation two nodes change to 1 Mbps data rate (slow-rate calls). The calls are considered to start with the G.711 codec and have the same duration. Monitoring frequency for the MAC monitor is set to 5 seconds, equal to the normal RTCP monitoring frequency. The fast RTCP transmission interval is set at 1 second, in order to minimize the reaction time of the algorithm. All users are considered to support all codecs and there is no other traffic or other interferences in the wireless network. Each STA has a queue length of $K = 50$ packets. The codecs used during simulations are the G.711, G.726, G.729 and G.723.1, ordered by their bitrate.

The network simulator $NS - 2$ [10] was used for the simulations, with the addition of the SIP module obtained from [11] in order to include the basic SIP agents. It was further adapted for the specific $NS - 2$ scenario with the goal of controlling the codec of each call while the call is in progress. The basic 802.11e MAC module was used, obtained from [12] with the default parameters set and the experiments were performed for different channel rates, from 1 to 11 Mbps.

4.1   Analysis

In order to understand the efficiency of the codec adaptation algorithm it is important to see what exactly happens to the network when no algorithm is present. When just two nodes start transmitting on a lower rate changing from 11 Mbps to 1 Mbps (at instant $t = 95$ on Figure 2), the packet loss percentage gets quickly very high, with values reaching almost 90%, which can be translated to call drop since almost all packets are lost. Moreover, the packet delay increases to very high values reaching 1 sec, as the queue length becomes saturated (Figure 3). The congestion of the system, both in terms of loss and delay, is much more obvious in the AP, since it aggregates the traffic of *all* calls, this is why we observe the difference on the results between uplink and downlink. The resulted saturation can be also observed from the very low throughput obtained in Figure 4.(b) and the low quality perceived by the user in the MOS calculation (Figure 4.(a)). The observed MOS, as calculated in real-time using the E-model, drops to values as low as 1, meaning communication breakdown according to the MOS standard definition. The situation is corrected only when one of the two nodes

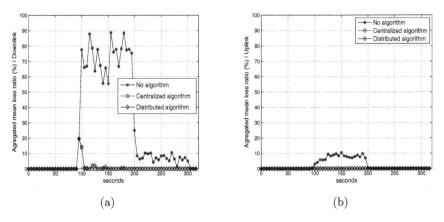

Fig. 2. Average aggregated packet loss percentage (a) Downlink (b) Uplink

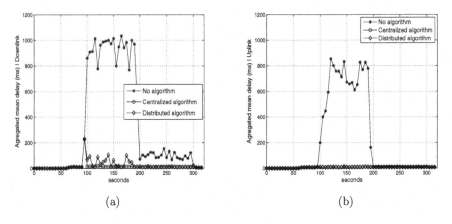

Fig. 3. Average aggregated Delay (a) Downlink (b) Uplink

that previously dropped to a lower rate change again to a higher rate (11 Mbps) at simulation instant $t = 200sec$. After this point, we observe a decrease on delay and packet loss, although they remain higher than the desired for a correct VoIP transmission, with delay above 100ms and packet loss percentage of 10% in the downlink.

The best solution is to lower the congestion level of the AP by reducing the codec of some of the calls. In the distributed implementation of the algorithm, almost instantly as the rate changes happen at $t = 95sec$ of the simulation, the nodes perceive the alarm situation and after a random waiting time they adapt to the network measurements by changing the codec. As we can see from the average throughput values obtained (figure 4.(b)), only some of the calls need to change codec and the transmission is re-stabilized very quickly, so while the total throughput may be lower than before the rate changes, since some calls now use codecs that require less bandwidth, the system is no longer saturated.

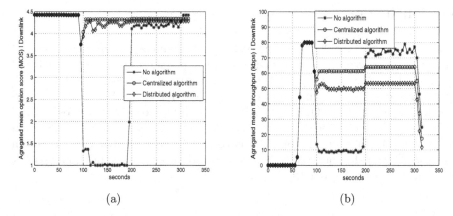

Fig. 4. (a) Average aggregated MOS (Downlink) (b) Average aggregated throughput (Downlink)

This can be verified in the packet loss and delay figures, where there is just one peak of high loss percentage reaching 20% and high delay of around 200 ms at the moment of the transmission rate changes, which are corrected immediately.

Even more impressive are the results of the centralized implementation. At the moment the MAC monitoring receives the rate change signal, it lowers by one the codec of the affected nodes. Along with this proactive codec change and by giving priority to the codec change on the calls that have suffered a rate drop, the total number of calls that need to change codec is lower than on the distributed implementation. This is evident from the total throughput obtained (Figure 4.(b)) which is higher than in the distributed mode, that is translated in more calls transmitting with higher bit rate codec. Again, both delay and packet loss results adjust to the expected performance as in the distributed implementation and even slightly better, with a peak at the moment of rate change which is fast corrected. During the rest of the time packet loss is practically 0 and delay remains on the order of a few milliseconds. The average MOS value, indicating the user perceived quality is maintained in very high values around 4.3, as can be seen in Figure 4.(a), with only an instant drop at the moment of the rate change and until the nodes start reacting. This shows a huge gain compared to the MOS with value less than 1.5 achieved when no algorithm is present.

As can be seen from the results, both implementations of the CAA give satisfactory performance, since no calls are being dropped, there is a fast reaction and correction of the quality degradation and there are minimal packet losses with high average MOS obtained. Comparing the centralized with the distributed implementation, it becomes clear that the centralized gives better results as expected, since the AP has an overall control of the nodes and the codec they use and provides a more efficient combination of codecs. On the other hand, this means more processing effort for the AP and the results on the distributed method are quite satisfactory and give an interesting and almost equally effective alternative to the centralized version.

5 Conclusions

In this work, the problem of a multi-rate environment on the voice over IP service was analyzed and as a solution two implementations, centralized and distributed, of the codec adaptation algorithm were proposed and compared. Based on cross-layer information from MAC and RTCP packets the algorithm can detect in real-time QoS problems on the voice flows and propose a new codec that adjusts better to the current conditions. As performance simulation results show, the algorithm proposed can solve efficiently the quality degradation provoked to the calls due to the rate changes, with no call drops, minimum packet losses and an average high MOS value.

References

1. Bellalta, B., Meo, M., Oliver, M.: A BEB-based Admission Control for VoIP calls in WLAN with coexisting elastic TCP flows. In: Koucheryavy, Y., Harju, J., Iversen, V.B. (eds.) NEW2AN 2006. LNCS, vol. 4003, Springer, Heidelberg (2006)
2. Heusse, M., Rousseau, F., Berger-Sabbatel, G., Duda, A.: RTP: Performance Anomaly of 802.11b. In: Proc. of IEEE INFOCOM 2003, San Francisco, USA (2003)
3. IEEE Std 802.11: Wireless LAN Medium Access Control (MAC) and Physical Layer (PHY) specifications. ANSI/IEEE Std 802.11, 1999 Edn. (Revised 2003)
4. IEEE Std 802.11e: Wireless LAN Medium Access Control (MAC) and Physical Layer (PHY) specifications. Amendment: Medium Access Control QoS enhancements, IEEE Std 802.11e (2005)
5. ITU-T Recommendation G.107: The E-model, a computational model for use in transmission planning (2000)
6. Jiwoong, J., Sunghyun, C., Chong-kwon, K.: Achieving Weighted Fairness between Uplink and Downlink in IEEE 802.11 DCF-Based WLANs. In: IEEE QShine'05, Orlando, USA (August 2005)
7. Kawata, T., Shin, S., Forte, A.G., Schulzrinne, H.: Using dynamic PCF to improve the capacity for VoIP traffic in IEEE 802.11 networks. In: IEEE Wireless Communications and Networking Conference, WCNC 2005, IEEE Computer Society Press, Los Alamitos (2005)
8. Lundberg, T., De Bruin, P., Bruhn, S., Hakansson, S., Craig, S.: Adaptive thresholds for AMR codec mode selection. IEEE, VTC Spring, Stockholm, Sweden (2005)
9. Manousos, M., et al.: Voice-Quality Monitoring and Control for VoIP. IEEE Internet Computing (July-August 2005)
10. Network Simulator-2: Version 2.28, http://www.isi.edu/nsnam/ns/
11. ns-2 SIP patch: National Institute of Standards and Technology (NIST)
12. ns-2 802.11e patch: Telecommunication Networks Group, Technical University of Berlin, Germany
13. Ott, et al.: Extended RTP Profile for RTCP-based Feedback (RTP/AVPF). Internet Draft (August 2004)
14. Qiao, Z., Sun, L., Heilemman, N., Ifeachor, E.: A new method for VoIP Quality of Service control use combined adaptive sender rate and priority marking. In: IEEE ICC'04, Paris, IEEE Computer Society Press, Los Alamitos (June 2004)

15. Sfairopoulou, A., Macián, C., Bellalta, B.: QoS adaptation in SIP-based VoIP calls in multi-rate IEEE 802.11 environments. In: IEEE ISWCS '06, Valencia, Spain, IEEE Computer Society Press, Los Alamitos (September 2006)
16. Sfairopoulou, A., Macián, C., Bellalta, B.: Dynamic measurement-based codec selection for VoIP in multirate IEEE 802.11 WLANs, Technical Report TD(07)018, Cost290 (February 2007), http://www.cost290.org
17. Tamura, T., Tadashi, I.: Wireless LAN Resource Management Mechanism Guaranteeing Minimum Available Bandwidth for Real-time Communication. In: IEEE WCNC 2005, New Orleans, USA, IEEE Computer Society Press, Los Alamitos (March 2005)
18. Trad, A., Ni, Q., Afifi, H.: Adaptive VoIP Transmission over Heterogeneous Wired/Wireless Networks. In: Roca, V., Rousseau, F. (eds.) MIPS 2004. LNCS, vol. 3311, Springer, Heidelberg (2004)

Decentralized Supplementary Services for Voice-over-IP Telephony

Christoph Spleiß and Gerald Kunzmann

Technische Universität München
80333 Munich, Germany
{christoph.spleiss,gerald.kunzmann}@tum.de

Abstract. As current Voice-over-IP (VoIP) systems encourage a direct communication between the callees they are similar in design to peer-to-peer (P2P) approaches. Therefore, we introduce a framework to build *distributed* supplementary services for VoIP. Some of these services like completion of calls on no reply or holding are already commonly established in public switched telephone networks or realized in centralized VoIP servers like Asterisk [1]. In order to foster the completely decentralization of these features we suggest corresponding services implemented on top of a structured P2P network. Using a resource-based approach new features can easily be deployed and announced.

Keywords: Voice over IP, telephony services, Peer-to-Peer, Framework.

1 Introduction

Supplementary services for telephony are a fixed part in today's communication world. Everybody uses features like call forwarding, completion of calls on non-reply or holding. These features are provided by a centralized local or private branch exchange. Due to centralization this approach has many disadvantages. Administration and maintenance of an exchange are very expensive as usually every terminal needs a separate line. Furthermore, in case of a breakdown every connected client is affected and the whole system will be unavailable.

In order to save costs and provide resilience, peer-to-peer technology (P2P) provides a reasonable approach to solve these problems. In this paper we describe how we can realize decentralized supplementary telephone services using a structured P2P system in a Voice-over-IP (VoIP) environment. We developed an extensible framework in which we can add supplementary telephone services to common VoIP systems like Skype or SIP. Furthermore, this approach is platform independent and can be used both on stationary and mobile devices.

The paper is organized as follows. Section 2 gives an introduction to P2P technology and a more detailed explanation of the structured P2P system CHORD. We also have a look at previous work done on a resource management framework (RMF) for P2P systems used in our approach. Afterwards we give an overview over supplementary telephony services in current public switched telephone networks which will be realized in our overlay network. Section 3 describes how

A. Pras and M. van Sinderen (Eds.): EUNICE 2007, LNCS 4606, pp. 62–69, 2007.

these services can be realized using CHORD and the RMF. Conclusions and directions for future work are presented in section 4.

1.1 P2P Systems

Compared to a client/server architecture like FTP, a pure P2P system hasn't got any central instance like a server. Every participant in such an environment acts both as a server providing data and storage, as well as a client, searching for content. Information is exchanged directly between the peers. Because every peer is sharing its own resources like storage space, a P2P system can store much more data than a single server. Also the data availability is higher than in a client/server system. In case of a breakdown of a few peers, only the data stored on them are lost. Even this risk can be minimized by using replication, that is storing the information on more than one node.

But the equality of all peers is not necessary in order to qualify a system as P2P. Napster for example uses a centralized indexing server to store references on the content of the whole P2P system and to provide a powerful lookup service. Every user willing to share data registers itself to the lookup-server and transmits a list of available files. Peers looking for a certain content gain the network address of peers with the desired content from the lookup-server. The file itself is directly transferred between the two peers. However, in case of lookup-servers' breakdown, the whole system isn't available any more.

Due to resilience problems of centralized P2P architectures the Gnutella protocol was developed which provides a fully decentralized architecture. Every peer holds a few connections to other peers. In order to search for content, queries are forwarded to all connected neighbours. Until the first match every peer forwards this query. To limit the packets' lifetime, a TTL counter is decremented at every hop. If the query is successful, the information is transmitted using the reverse path of the query.

Because of the high bandwidth consumption of Gnutella hierarchical topologies like Fasttrack were developed. As a hybrid P2P system, Fasttrack provides so called supernodes, which form a Gnutella network, and so called leafnodes, which are connected to one of the supernodes. Fasttrack provides the high resilience of Gnutella combined with the bandwidth efficiency of Napster.

All P2P architectures described above belong to the so called unstructured P2P systems. The next generation in P2P systems are structured P2P systems [2], [3] like CHORD [6] which are based on the principle of distributed hash tables (DHT) to provide efficient routing mechanisms. CHORD has got a circular structure whereby specific node features are used to calculate a n-bit hash value m for every node. According to the hash value the nodes are arranged in a circle. The same hashing function is used to provide a key k for the content stored in the network. Every key k is now assigned to the first node whose identifier is greater than or equal to k. To provide routing and lookup mechanisms every peer maintains a routing table with entries pointing to at least its direct successor and predecessor in the ring. To make lookups much faster, CHORD also maintains an additional routing table, the so-called *finger table*. The finger table has got n entries, where each entry i points to the node first that succeeds m by at least 2^{i-1}. These fingers are used to provide shortcuts through the ring during the lookup process. Because the distance to a key k will be at least halved in every step, each query can be resolved in $\mathcal{O}(logN)$ hops, where N is the number of participating nodes.

1.2   Resource Management Framework for P2P Networks

In order to define a structure to our content stored in the P2P network we use the idea of metadata representation shown in [4]. Every content needs certain properties to build a defined structure. The mandatory property of a content is the `type` descriptor as it determines the semantic interpretation of further properties. In addition, every content is identified by a unique identifier (`UID`). This `UID` is provided by our DHT function. Links between contents are created by storing the UID of another content in the `linkUID` property.

1.3   Supplementary Telephony Services in Public Switched Telephone Networks (PSTN)

Common communication carriers provide their customers a great variety of supplementary telephony services [5]. These services are realized on centralized exchanges with all disadvantages mentioned before. These supplementary services are for example:

- **Calling Line Identification Presentation/Restriction** is a telephony network service that transmits the caller's telephone number to the called party or blocks the transmission. The state for the indication is set by the caller and evaluated in the telephone exchange. The exchange is responsible for proceeding the correct information to the called party.
- **Completion of Calls to Busy Subscribers/on No Reply** is a telephony network service that allows the calling party to automate the call origination in the telephone exchange for the unavailable subscriber. Because the exchange as a centralized instance knows the state of every participant, it can initiate the callback if the desired destination is available again.
- **Call Waiting** is a feature that a subscriber gets a audio signal during an active connection signaling that another party wants to establish a connection. The called party doesn't get the congestion signal but the ringing signal. The party informed by the audio signal can decide if the waiting call should be rejected, accepted by terminating the current call or accepted by putting the current call on hold.
- **Call forwarding** is a feature where an incoming phone call is redirected to another party. The diversion can occur immediately, after a certain time or if the called party is busy.
- **Three-Party-Conference** is a feature whereby a party can establish a conference between itself and two other parties. Afterwards every party can hear the others at the same time. This feature is normally controlled by

the telephone exchange but can also be provided by the end device of the originator. In the last case the originator needs at least two phone lines.

- **Hold** is a telephony network feature where during a call a party can put the remote party on hold. The party on hold is receiving music on hold from the exchange. The initiated party has the possibility to switch to another phone and resume the connection. This procedure has to be finished within a certain time, otherwise the connection to the party on hold will be terminated by the exchange.

Some of the features shown above are to be realized with a CHORD P2P System. In the next section we will see which features can be realized in the P2P network itself and which have to be realized in the end devices.

2 Implementing Supplementary Services Using P2P Technology

Our goal is to provide an overlay network for supplementary telephony services which integrates already common VoIP solutions like Skype or SIP. We do not need to develop an own channel for voice transmission as the overlay is an additional feature to existing communication solutions. This project shall be realized using the basic functions provided by a P2P network: storing and finding of information. In our implementation we used CHORD as the underlying P2P network. Also any other structured P2P network is applicable. The supplementary services are provided on top of this protocol. However, it is not possible to realize all services shown above solely in the P2P network. Thus, calling line identification presentation is a service which can only be provided by the end device, because the communication takes place on a direct P2P connection without an exchange in between. Also three party conference has to be realized directly in the end device as there's no exchange to merge the speech signals. In addition, services are expected to work cross platform, i.e. both mobile and stationary end devices should be able to use services provided by the overlay.

2.1 Searching Subscribers

Before communication can start we have to ensure that subscribers can find each other. As interaction between different VoIP systems is desired we cannot directly use Skype or SIP URIs but we have to develop our own lookup process inside the P2P network. For these purposes every subscriber has to enter individual-related data like given name, family name and email address into his end device. Also a dialplan has to be created which will be discussed in the next subsection. The end device is computing five hash values, one used as the UID for the content type called *contact sheet*, and the others used as the UID for four contents of type *profile*. The profiles contain the full name of the subscriber and a linkUID to the contact sheet. They are hashed with the subscriber's given name, family name, both names together and email address (Fig. 1) and then published in the

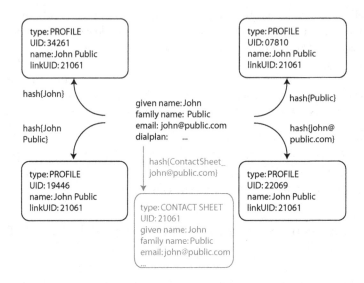

Fig. 1. Four profiles generated out of the users data

P2P network. We are using personal information about the subscriber to hash our profiles so that subscribers searching for others can enter something they know about the desired party like the family name into their end device. After calculating the UID out of the search string, this value is committed to the P2P network which will return all profiles matching the search key. If the desired party has been returned and selected by the user, the contact sheet referred in the linkUID-field of the profile is obtained. As the contact sheet contains the dialplan a connection to the other party can be established according to the dialplan.

2.2   Dialplan and Call Forwarding

The dialplan is the most important component necessary during the origination. Every subscriber needs to enter a set of rules how he wants to be accessible (via Skype, SIP or others) and in which order. Also a timeout value for every dialplan rule is necessary. If a rule isn't successful within the given timeout value, the next rule will be attempted. The dialplan length is arbitrary as it can be realized as a linked list. This dialplan is saved inside the contact sheet together with further user information such as the users IP-address and a time stamp of the last update (Fig. 2). The UID value for the contact sheet is determined out of the user's email address with the prefix "ContactSheet_". This salted hash is necessary as we already use the hash obtained by the email address for a profile's UID. Based on the fact than an email address is unique there shouldn't be any collisions between contact sheets. After the reception of a contact sheet the recipient tries to establish a connection according to the dialplan. The dialplan is subjected to be changed at any time by the owner. Changes occur immediately

```
type: CONTACT SHEET
UID: 21061
given name: John
family name: Public
email: max@mustermann.de
update: 2006-08-31 12:08:21 GMT+1
IP: 129.187.54.67
Dialplan:    Skype:john_office; 30
             Skype:john_home; 20
             SIP:12345@sip.com; 60
```

Fig. 2. Contact sheet with dialplan attached

as the contact sheet is reloaded at every connection attempt. If a speech system isn't supported by the caller the next eligible rule is taken. This is also the way how we realized the supplementary feature call forwarding. After certain time the next dialplan rule is chosen. In order to provide immediate call forwarding the user is able to select zero as timeout value. This rule will be skipped.

2.3   Completion of Calls on No Reply

This supplementary feature is realized with content of the so called type info profile. If no rule in the dialplan of a subscriber was successful, the caller has the opportunity to send a call-back request to the unavailable subscriber. For this purpose the caller generates a info profile of the category call-back which has the same UID as the contact sheet of the unavailable person and publishes it in the P2P network (Fig. 3, left). Furthermore the info profile contains a time stamp, the caller's name and a linkUID to it's contact sheet in order to initiate the call-back.

Every subscriber connected to the overlay periodically checks if there are any info profiles existing for his UID. This is possible because the info profile's UID is known and can be queried. If a subscriber receives a call-back info profile he can choose if he wants to establish the call-back or ignore the request. He can also use multiple devices to receive this info profile as the application is platform independent. In both cases the info profile is deleted after it has been received to avoid multiple notifications of the same event. The major difference between the same service provided by telephone exchanges is that the call-back is not established by the exchange but by the other party.

2.4   Putting Calls on Hold

Like the supplementary service completion of calls on no reply the service putting calls on hold is realized with info profiles. Subscribers having an active connection can put the other party on hold in order to resume the call from another location. To achieve this the hold initiating subscriber generates an info profile of category on-hold. This info profile also contains a time stamp, the UID of the initiators own contact sheet, the full name of the subscriber which is put on hold and the

```
type: INFO
UID: 21061
category: call-back
timestamp: 2007-03-19 13:42:08 GMT+1
caller name: John Public
contact hash: 32563
```

```
type: INFO
UID: 21061
category: on-hold
timestamp: 2007-03-19 13:42:08 GMT+1
user on hold: John Public
voice channel: Skype: john_office
```

Fig. 3. Call-back and on-hold info profile

last active voice channel (Fig. 3, right). After this, the info profile is published in the P2P network and the active communication is disconnected.

The initiating subscriber has now again the opportunity to change its end device, e.g. from a PC to a PDA. As soon as the new device is connected to the P2P network it checks for relevant info profiles. If an info profile with on-hold information is received, the user can decide if he wants to reestablish the former connection with the same voice channel used before. The info profile is deleted after reception.

3   Summary and Outlook

We have shown that it is possible to provide supplementary telephony services without the need of a centralized instance using only P2P technology. In addition, we have developed a Java-client connected to Skype via the SkypeAPI and to a CHORD P2P network which provides all services shown above. Although Skype is proprietary we have chosen this speech system as it provides an easy to use API and sufficient possibilities to control and monitor call states. Anyway we do not use the supplementary services offered by Skype as other systems may not support them and we want to make the services usable in all imlemented speech systems. This makes is necessary to implement another speech system like SIP to utilize the possibilities of the framework.

Using the resource management framework new features can easily be implemented by simply defining new info profiles for new supplementary services. Possible ideas are for example voice gateways which can convert the speech signal from one VoIP system to another, i.e. from Skype to SIP. Info profiles are used to propagate the existence of these gateway and to announce their facilities. Other services are enhanced messaging services which collect the info profiles of registered subscribers and inform them about events via email or SMS. Also, reminder services and distributed calendars are easy to implement.

In order to protect the overlay from malpractice some security features still need to be integrated. We suggest a PKI based approach as it must be guaranteed that nobody is inserting malicious info profiles or removes info profiles and contact sheets without permission.

References

1. Asterisk: An open source PBX and telephony toolkit, Digium, http://www.asterisk.org
2. Eberspächer, J., Schollmeier, R., Zöls, S., Kunzmann, G.: Structured P2P Networks in Mobile and Fixed Environments. In: Proceedings of HET-NETs '04 International Working Conference on Performance Modelling and Evaluation of Heterogeneous Networks 2004, Ilkley (2004)
3. Kellerer, W., Kunzmann, G., Schollmeier, R., Zöls, S.: Structured Peer-to-Peer Systems for Telecommunications and Mobile Environments. AEÜ - International Journal of Electronics and Communications (2006)
4. Friese, T., Freisleben, B., Rusitschka, S., Southall, A.: A Framework for Resource Management in Peer-to-Peer Networks. Department of Mathematics and Computer Science, University of Marburg
5. Siemens Communication Lexicon: Siemens Enterprise Communications GmbH & Co. KG, http://networks.siemens.com/communications/lexicon_en/index.htm
6. Stoica, I., Morris, R., Liben-Nowell, D., Karger, D., Kaashoek, M., Dabek, F., Balakrishnan, H.: Chord: A Scalable Peer-to-peer Lookup Service for Internet Applications. In: Proceedings of the 2001 SIGCOMM conference, ACM Press, New York (2001)

Analysis of Techniques for Protection Against Spam over Internet Telephony

Vincent M. Quinten, Remco van de Meent, and Aiko Pras

University of Twente, The Netherlands
v.m.quinten@student.utwente.nl,
{r.vandemeent, a.pras}@utwente.nl

Abstract. Spam in Internet telephony (SPIT) networks is likely to become a large problem in the future, as more and more people and companies switch from traditional telephone networks to Voice over IP (VoIP) networks, and as it is easy to spam VoIP users. The goal of this survey paper is to identify techniques to prevent and reduce SPIT. To compare the various SPIT protection techniques, criteria will be presented that must be met by these techniques. We also identify several combinations of techniques that complement each other, to increase the protection effectiveness.

1 Introduction

Spam over Internet telephony (SPIT) is defined as unsolicited bulk calls that result in media sessions, of which the content delivered to phone or voice terminals may include voice, images and / or video [1]. There are several kinds of SPIT, i.e. advertisement, telephone poll and telemarketing. Voice over Internet Protocol (VoIP) usage is growing fast; it is estimated that in the year 2010 25% of all households in Western Europe have abandoned traditional Public Switched Telephone Network (PSTN) services in favour of VoIP [2]. With the growth of VoIP communication, the 'abuse' of VoIP will grow as well. Advertisers who send numerous voicemail messages to VoIP users will cause a reduction in bandwidth and possible failures of the service, and are annoying for VoIP users. Compared to e-mail spam, the load on network resources by SPIT may be ten times as much [3]. SPIT is also more obtrusive [4], because the phone will ring with every spam message, even in the middle of the night, disturbing the users current activity. The use of VoIP instead of traditional PSTN networks will make it easier for spammers to make automated tools to deliver their spam to the user [1] and VoIP communication is also much cheaper, often flat-rate. The authors of [5] claim that the costs per call for VoIP are roughly three orders of magnitude lower than traditional PSTN calls, making it a lot cheaper for a spammer to get his message out into the world.

The two main protocols for VoIP are the H.323 protocol and the Session Initiation Protocol (SIP). Because of implementation errors and protocol features that may be exploited, both protocols will be equally vulnerable for SPIT [6]. Because of this, no distinction will be made between both protocols in the remainder of this paper.

Goal. This survey paper presents the state of the art of techniques to prevent or mitigate spam in VoIP networks. The paper discusses the various techniques and identifies

A. Pras and M. van Sinderen (Eds.): EUNICE 2007, LNCS 4606, pp. 70–77, 2007.

which combinations of techniques may be most promising for the future. This survey can be used as a reference to other researchers who want to develop new SPIT prevention techniques or improve existing techniques. Such paper was not available at the time of writing. However, two papers exist which discuss some related work. In [5] some techniques are discussed together with their advantages and disadvantages; that paper, however, only contains a small selection of spam protection techniques and aims at SIP techniques. A selection of the techniques described in the present paper is also described in [7], but [7] does not provide criteria upon which an analysis could be based.

Approach and organization. To provide this state of the art, a study of existing literature on the topic of SPIT has been conducted. Section 2 describes the criteria that SPIT prevention techniques have to meet; these criteria have been extracted from the literature. Section 3 lists the techniques, together with their main advantages and disadvantages. Section 4 provides an analysis of the effectiveness of these techniques, using the criteria from section 2. Finally section 5 contains some conclusions and remarks.

2   Criteria

For SPIT mitigation techniques to be effective and user friendly, they need to meet a number of criteria. This section discusses the most important criteria that have been distilled from literature on the topic of SPIT.

An important criterion is that protection techniques have to identify spam before the user's phone rings [1]. Because every time the phone rings it disturbs the user's current activity, spam is extremely annoying, particularly if the user wakes up in the middle of the night. A second criterion relates to maintenance of the protection technique. The less maintenance is needed by the user, the better [4]. So ideally the SPIT protection technique should be transparent to the user, which means that preferably it must be located at the service provider. The cost involved with spam protection is also an important aspect. Preferably the costs for the user are as low as possible, but the costs for the spammer should be as high as possible to assure that spamming becomes less profitable, which may eventually reduce the amount of spam [8]. The delay of the call caused by the protection technique is also an important factor to consider [4,8]. The less delay caused by the technique, the better; preferably the technique should not cause any delay at all, because long delays harm the direct nature of a telephone conversation. Another important issue is the impossibility to bypass spam blocking by spammers. Each spam protection technique will totally fail if spammers become able to circumvent the blocking [8]. A good spam protection technique should therefore be both effective as well as difficult to circumvent. Finally, the number of false positives and false negatives should be as small as possible, preferably even zero. This is important, because for many businesses and home users, telephone calls are very important. For businesses it's even essential that potential customers can reach the company [1].

3   Techniques

Based on the criteria defined in the previous section, this section discusses a number of techniques, including their advantages and disadvantages:

Signaling Protocol Analysis. VoIP calls consist of two parts: signaling and media data. Before a VoIP call starts, signaling data for setting up the call is exchanged between both users. Spammers are interested in the correct delivery of their calls, therefore the call routing information provided in the call setup request is valid and can therefore be used for further analysis. A characteristic of spam calls is that they are unidirectional: the spammer initiates the calls to the targeted network, but in general nobody calls the spammer. Another characteristic is the termination behavior; this is statistically consistent, so calls are generally terminated by the same party. A final distinction is that spammers in general do not call the same recipient for some period of time. Based on these characteristics, the authors of [1] defined a number of scenarios for termination behavior. Based on a statistical analysis of this behavior, the authors claim that it is possible to detect spammers with an accuracy of about 99.9%.

This technique has the benefits that it decides if a call is a spam call before the phone at the receiving side rings and the technique is located at the service provider, so the user isn't bothered with spam calls and maintenance. However this technique can only decide if a call is a spam call after at least ten calls from one caller. This indicates a heavy reliance on the fact that a spammer will not change his number for quite some time. But in reality it is quite easy to change your number in VoIP systems, this will make this technique relatively easy to circumvent. *Signaling protocol analysis* will also block some legitimate services, for example an automated system of the bookstore to inform you, your book has arrived. However this technique is fairly new, there is only one article [1] published about *signaling protocol analysis* to prevent spam in VoIP networks.

Do Not Call Registers are agreements between telemarketers that have agreed on that they will not call users that registered their phone number. Such a register can be controlled nationwide, so the user only has to register his phone number on one place and the control organization will handle the rest of the administration, so user maintenance is minimal [9]. This control organization also gives penalties to telemarketers who don't obey their agreement, this enforces the effectiveness of the register [10]. But a big disadvantage of *do not call registers* is, that it's an agreement of telemarketers, when a telemarketer has no agreement with the do not call register he can still spam registered users, this also holds for outsourced spam sources off-shore [1]. Off-shore spam sources are not very unlikely, because the costs for calling to another country are much less compared with the costs for normal PSTN calls. In contrast the costs involved with maintaining the do not call register and the investigation of complains can be high. These costs are eventually paid by the TAX payer instead of the spammer [10].

Circles of trust, as described in [5], is another technique that is very similar to a do not call register. Companies agree to exchange VoIP calls amongst each other and also agree to introduce a fine should one of them being caught spamming. Each company enacts measures to terminate employees who spam from their account. Circles of trust work well on small domains, but it is unknown how they would scale in large domains.

Whitelisting is a technique primarily used in instant messaging networks. In case of VoIP a whitelist contains the telephone numbers of the people that are allowed to call you, all other people are blocked. *Whitelisting* blocks all spam calls in theory, assuming nobody on your whitelist is a spam source or will become one [7]. But this is also a big disadvantage, because if a unknown person wants to call you, his call will be blocked. Some home users don't think this is a disadvantage, but for business users it is vital that potential customers are able to contact them [7].

Whitelists are difficult to circumvent [5], because a change of identity will have no use. They also give the user complete control over who can and who can't call them, but this comes at a price. When users receive often calls from new callers, the amount of maintenance to the whitelist can be considerable.

Blacklisting is the complete opposite of *whitelisting*, instead of maintaining a list of numbers of the people that are allowed to call you, you maintain a list of numbers that aren't. For this system to be effective it needs to be implemented on a global level, when separate users maintain their one blacklists it will have very limited effects, because spammers will simply call someone else. Only on a global scale the costs for spammers can raise that much that spamming becomes unprofitable [7]. However everybody should be able to add a number to the blacklist, so a non-profit organization is needed to maintain the blacklist [7]. But even on a global scale it will not prevent users from receiving spam, because before a number is added to the blacklist a certain number of users have to answer the call and file a complaint and as mentioned before it's very easy to change your number in VoIP systems [5,7]. The use of proxy's in combination with blacklists also cause some unwanted side effects, because every user behind a proxy will be blocked when it is added to the blacklist, not just the spammer [5,7].

Greylisting applies a simple rule to all incoming calls: each call will be blocked, unless the same number has tried to establish a call within the last N hours/minutes. When a call is blocked, the sender will receive a message like "the user is currently busy". When the sender calls again within the N hour timeframe, his number is automatically added to a whitelist and all future calls will be connected immediately, requiring very little work from users [8]. *Greylisting* will not suffer from false positives when the used VoIP protocols are implemented correctly [7,8] and it will increase the costs for the spammer because he needs to call every user at least twice within the timeframe to make a successful call [7], which are great benefits.

According to [8], trying to circumvent *greylisting* has no effect or even an opposed effect, because *greylisting* will make other techniques even more effective, but we believe that spammers will adopt their systems to call twice within the timeframe. The delay caused by the rejection of the first call attempt makes *greylisting* unsuitable for most business users and emergency or other urgent calls [7].

A techniques similar to *greylisting* is described in [11]. Consent based communication, as described in [5], is also similar, except for automatically adding numbers to the whitelist, this causes an extra way to circumvent the technique by flooding the users with consent requests instead of spam calls [5].

Rate limiting allows the user to make a certain amount of calls per day. When the user exceeds the limit, he is likely to be a spam source and will be blocked. This simple technique doesn't bother average users, but will limit spammers [7]. But it has to be supported by all service providers worldwide, because otherwise spammers will just switch to a more spam-friendly provider [7].

Reputation filtering is a system adopted from instant messaging, where users can give each other reputation scores, based on this score users can decide to allow or reject a call. When a call is allowed the number is added to a whitelist, comparable to buddy lists in instant messaging networks. However spammers are able to cheat in large networks by helping each other to receive a good reputation, which makes the system useless [5]. And the delay caused by reputation search paths can become very long in large networks which is not preferable [12]. As pointed out earlier with *whitelisting* user maintenance can become intensive [12].

Handshake/Challenge/Turing Tests, further referred to as *Turing tests*, is a technique adopted from e-mail and depends on the fact that some things are easy for humans, but almost impossible for computers [5]. However there is evidence that there are systems that can circumvent this technique, like described in [13]. In VoIP systems a user could answer a spoken question, for example a little math question and when the user provides the correct answer he is instantly connected [5]. Since speech recognition is difficult for computers with today's technology this will hold of automated spam calls. Added benefit in contrast with *greylisting* and *memory bound functions* the call will not lose its instant character [7]. But the system will not be very well suited for internationalization, because of the spoken question and the technique relies heavily on user acceptance making it not very attractive for business users [7].

Payments-at-risk tries to make spam more expensive for the spammer, but minimize the costs for the user. To achieve this, the calling party has to make a small deposit to the called party before the calling party can make the call, which will be refunded when the called party doesn't mark the call as being spam [5]. The problem with this system is that the costs for micro payment transactions make normal users lose money on every call. An example in [5] calculates that this will cost a normal user about $1.95 a month, when the user receives about 10 calls a day from unknown senders, which is relatively inexpensive.

Content Filtering makes use of speech recognition technology to analyze if the content of a message is spam, however with today's technology it's impossible to analyze the content real-time [5]. The system kicks in when the user has already answered the phone and is already disturbed by the spam call making the system ineffective, but it could be used to analyze voicemail messages. However VoIP providers that use some kind of encryption for extra security [14] or spammers trying to circumvent the system by using bad grammar or an accent [5] will provide even more difficulties for *content filtering* and probably even cause the technique to fail.

Memory Bound Functions. The basic idea of *memory bound functions* is: "If I don't know you and you want to send me a message, then you must prove that you spent, say, ten seconds of CPU time, just for me and just for this message" [15]. This "proof of effort" is mainly cryptographic, it's hard to compute but very easy to check. This "proof of effort" will consume computing power at the senders' device for every call, which implies that a spammer needs much more hardware for the same amount of calls and also has to pay the extra calling costs [7]. Average users will not be bothered by the small delay introduced according to [7] and normal calls will not be blocked, so it is still possible to make legal advertisement calls [7]. However for urgent calls and emergency calls the system is completely unacceptable [7].

4 Effectiveness Analysis

This section combines the results from the previous two sections and contains an effectiveness analysis for the techniques described before. The criterion of false positives and false negatives could not be considered, because at the time of writing no figures on this where available.

Unsuitable techniques. We identified *content filtering*, *do not call registers*, *reputation filtering*, *rate limiting* and *blacklisting* as being unsuitable techniques to prevent VoIP spam, because they don't meet the criteria defined in section 2. *Content filtering*, *blacklisting* and *rate-limiting* don't work before the phone rings, so they still allow disturbance of the users current activity. *Blacklisting* and *reputation filtering* additionally need a lot of maintenance when calls are received from many different sources. For *blacklisting* to be effective, implementation on a global scale is necessary, but this involves high costs for maintenance and control. *Do not call registers* also suffer from high maintenance costs; these costs will eventually be paid by the receiver of spam and not by the spammer. Reputation filters cause long delays when used in large networks, degrading the instant character of telephone communications.

Rate-limiting, *content filtering* and *blacklisting* are not feasible, because they respectively only limit the spammer in their ability, need technology that's not available and cause unwanted side-effects. Furthermore, all these techniques suffer from the fact that they are easy to circumvent.

Techniques with potential. The techniques that, in our opinion, show potential to become a suitable technique against SPIT or that will be effective in combination with other techniques are *whitelisting*, *signaling protocol analysis*, *payments at risk*, *greylisting* and *Turing tests*. The authors of [1] claim that *signaling protocol analysis* should have an effectiveness of about 99.9%; if this claim holds in practice, this would be a very good technique, but practical tests need to be done. A technique that's also very effective, but requires a lot of maintenance is *whitelisting*. *Whitelisting* is a qualified as a potential technique, because it shows some nice properties when used in combination with other techniques. *Greylisting* is a technique that needs to be used in combination with other techniques by design and it aims at raising the costs for spammers, because the spammer needs to call everyone at least twice. A main disadvantage of *greylisting* is the delay it causes, so it's not suitable for urgent or emergency calls. *Payments at risk* also raise the costs at the place it really hurts, at the spammer, thus make spamming less profitable and therefore reduce the amount of spam in the future. *Turing tests*, on the other hand, try to ensure a spammer has a hard time meeting the challenge presented to him; when a spammer succeeds to circumvent the *Turing tests*, it's easy to make the question more difficult. However, *Turing tests* require a certain amount of knowledge, which can be a problem when, for example, a child tries to call her father at work and is presented with the question "What is the capital of Italy?". Also, when the question becomes more difficult, the checking of the answer may become more difficult. If the buttons of the telephone are no longer sufficient to provide the answer, speech recognition may seem to be a solution. But, as described before, speech recognition is still unfeasible with today's technology.

Suitable techniques. The only technique that fulfills most criteria and is therefore in our opinion suitable, is *memory bound functions*. *Memory bound functions* work before the phone rings, increase the costs for spammers and are located at the service provider, thus are completely transparent to the end-user. The only criterion that isn't met by *memory bound functions*, is that it causes a small delay in all calls, but this can be solved easily, as will be described in the next section.

Combination of techniques. Using combinations of techniques can cancel out most of the disadvantages of the stand-alone techniques. The combinations we identified are *Turing tests* together with *whitelisting*, *memory bound functions* with *whitelisting* or *signaling protocol analysis* with *whitelisting*. In combination with the first two techniques, *whitelisting* reduces the delay, because the challenge or "proof of effort" needs to be done only once; afterwards the number of the caller is added to the whitelist and further challenges are skipped. This also partially solves the knowledge problem with *Turing tests*. A possible disadvantage of this combination, however, can be that spammers will adapt to the system [7], but this could be resolved by adding an expiration time to the entries on the whitelist.

Whitelists in combination with *signaling protocol analysis* reduces the amount of false positives [1], because automated services like the one of the bookstore described earlier could be added to the whitelist.

5   Concluding Remarks

In this paper we have identified a number of protection mechanisms to prevent SPIT. These techniques can be divided into 4 categories: unsuitable techniques, techniques with potential, suitable techniques and combinations of techniques. In this paper the following techniques have been categorized as unsuitable: *content filtering*, *do not call registers*, *reputation filtering*, *rate limiting* and *blacklisting*. The following techniques have been categorized as having potential: *whitelisting*, *signaling protocol analysis*, *payments-at-risk*, *greylisting* and *Turing tests*. One technique is categorized as being suitable: *memory bound functions*. This technique fulfills almost all criteria defined in section 2 and is therefore suitable for use. *Turing tests* in combination with *whitelisting*, *memory bound functions* in combination with *whitelisting*, as well as *signaling protocol analysis* in combination with *whitelisting* are combinations that cancel out almost all disadvantages of each other.

There is not a single technique or combination of techniques that is the most promising approach for the future, but there are several options. Practical tests with these techniques need to be conducted to show which technique(s) will be best for use.

SPIT protection will probably always stay an arms race between spammers that try to circumvent protection techniques and researchers that develop new techniques or improve existing ones. However, as shown in this paper, by combining multiple VoIP spam protection techniques, many of the disadvantages can be canceled out.

We conclude with some remarks on possible future research. Most of the described techniques are easy to circumvent, just because it's easy to change your identity/phone number in VoIP networks. To prevent this kind of circumvention, research could be done to improve the system that allows someone to request new numbers. The effectiveness of almost all VoIP spam prevention techniques would benefit from this. Measuring effectiveness is also a subject that needs further research, as for most described techniques no real test data is available regarding their effectiveness. To verify the various techniques, practical tests need to be conducted to draw better conclusions on which techniques are effective in practice. The *Turing test* technique also needs further research, the determine how to overcome the language barrier when the system is used in an international context.

References

1. MacIntosh, R., Vinokurov, D.: Detection and mitigation of spam in IP telephony networks using signalling protocol analysis, pp. 49–52 (2005)
2. ElectricNews.Net. Mobile and VoIP to inherit the earth (15-09-2006): The Register (2005) http://www.theregister.co.uk/2005/06/27/rising_mobile_voip_revenues
3. Gagner, R.P.: Voice over Internet protocol: Secure or not recommendations to the business and private sector. Bowie State University, Maryland (2005)
4. Pessage, J., Seedorf, J.: Voice over IP: Unsafe at any Bandwidth? In: Eurescom Summit Heidelberg (2005)
5. Rosenberg, J., Jennings, C.: The Session Initiation Protocol (SIP) and SPAM. In: Internet Draft (2004)
6. Edelson, E.: Voice over IP: security pitfalls. Network Security, vol. 2005, pp. 4–7 (2005)
7. Radermacher, T.A.: Spam Prevention in Voice over IP Networks. University of Salzburg, Salzburg (2005)
8. Harris, E.: The Next Step in the Spam Control War: Greylisting (24-09-2006), Evan Harris (2003), http://projects.puremagic.com/greylisting/whitepaper.html
9. Federal Trade Commission: National Do Not Call Registry (14-09-2006) (2005), http://www.ftc.gov/donotcall/
10. Edwards, T.: A Review of Southern States' No-Call Registries. In: Southern Legislative Conference Atlanta (2002)
11. Croft, N.J., Olivier, M.S.: A Model for Spam Prevention in IP Telephony Networks using Anonymous Verifying Authorities. In: ISSA 2005 New Knowledge Today Conference, South Africa (2005)
12. Rebahi, Y., Sisalem, D.: SIP Service Providers and The Spam Problem. In: Voice over IP Security Workshop, Washington (2005)
13. Hocevar, S.: PWNtcha - captcha decoder (20-12-2006) (2005), http://sam.zoy.org/pwntcha/
14. Skype: Skype Help. (23-11-2006) (2006) support.skype.com
15. Cynthia, D., Andrew, G., Moni, N.: On Memory-Bound Functions for Fighting Spam (2003)

A Reputation-Based Approach for Securing Vivaldi Embedding System

Damien Saucez, Benoit Donnet, and Olivier Bonaventure

Université Catholique de Louvain, CSE Department

Abstract. Many large-scale Internet applications optimize their overlay network to reduce latencies. Embedding coordinate systems like Vivaldi are valuable tools for this new range of applications since they propose light-weight algorithms that permit to estimate the latency between any pair of nodes without having to contact them first. It has been recently demonstrated that coordinate systems in general and Vivaldi in particular are sensible to attacks. Typically, nodes can lie about their coordinate and distort the coordinate space. In this paper, we propose a formal reputation model to detect misbehaving nodes and propose a reputation adaptation of Vivaldi called RVivaldi. We evaluate the performance of RVivaldi using the King dataset and show that RVivaldi is less sensitive to malicious nodes than Vivaldi.

1 Introduction

During the last few years, many different application-level overlays have been proposed to support new range of applications from file sharing to Voice over IP (VoIP) and, more recently, IPTV. Most of these applications rely on the network delay or round-trip times (RTTs) to ensure quality of service (QoS). To limit resources consumption of the proximity measures, Internet coordinate systems have been proposed to allow hosts to estimate delays without doing direct measurements [1,2,3]. Every node of an Internet coordinate system computes its coordinates into a geometric space such that the distance from itself to any host predicts the latency – called *distance* – to that node. Ledlie et al. [4] have shown coordinate systems are valuable tools for distributed systems depending on the topology of the network. However, due to their slow convergence, coordinate systems must be deployed as always-on services available for higher level applications.

Content distribution and file sharing systems can benefit from network coordinates in order to select a number of replicated servers to fetch a data item from. *Azureus*, for instance, was the first large-scale real world application to use a coordinate system. Open-source widely spread systems like Azureus may interest attackers. One can imagine modifying Azureus client to alter the coordinate space and disrupt the whole service or controlling all the traffic to achieve a denial-of-service (DoS) attack.

Large-scale always-on services are prime target for attackers as disruption may result in a mis-functioning of many applications or overlay. Kaafar et al. have recently demonstrated that coordinate systems are sensible to attacks [5].

A. Pras and M. van Sinderen (Eds.): EUNICE 2007, LNCS 4606, pp. 78–85, 2007.

Kaafar et al. [5] have proposed to separate attacks on coordinate systems in different categories. To summarize, one can say that there are two kinds of attacks. The first one is performed when an honest node asks coordinates to a malicious one. The malicious node replies with false coordinates resulting in a bad latency prediction. Secondly, attackers disrupt the coordinates computation process itself resulting in a deformation of the space of both honest and malicious nodes (i.e., the predicted distances of the entire system are altered).

In this paper, we propose an extension to Vivaldi, called *Reputation-based Vivaldi* (RVivaldi), that ensures the security of Vivaldi. The key idea of RVivaldi is to add two new types of entities in the system: The *RCA*, a certificating agent, and the *surveyors* that estimate the reputation of the classic nodes. We propose a formal model of RVivaldi and validate it using the King data set used in [3]. We show that RVivaldi leads to a better accuracy of the coordinates than Vivaldi in presence of malicious nodes.

The remainder of this paper is organized as follows: Sec. 2 gives a brief overview of Vivaldi, the embedding system on which this paper is based; Sec. 3 presents our reputation model for embedding systems and its application to Vivaldi; Sec. 4 evaluates our solution. Finally, Sec. 5 summarizes this paper and discusses further works.

2   Vivaldi

Vivaldi [3] does not require a fixed network infrastructure and make no distinctions between nodes. A Vivaldi node collects distance information for a couple of neighbors and computes its new coordinates with the collected measures. The idea is that node i is represented as a unitary mass connected to each neighbor j by a spring with the rest length set to the measured RTT (d_{ij}). The actual length of the spring is the distance ($\hat{d}_{ij}$) predicted by the coordinate space. A spring always tries to have an actual length equals to its rest length. Thus if $\hat{d}_{ij}$ is smaller than the measured RTT, the spring will push the two masses attached to it. On the contrary, if the spring is too long, it will pull the masses and reduce its actual length. The coordinates in Vivaldi are updated following this principle. If we note $\overrightarrow{x}_i$ the coordinates of i and $\overrightarrow{x}_j$ the coordinates of j, the new coordinates are computed as follows:

$$\overrightarrow{x}_i = \overrightarrow{x}_i + \delta \cdot \left(d_{ij} - \hat{d}_{ij} \right) \cdot u \left(\overrightarrow{x}_i - \overrightarrow{x}_j \right). \tag{1}$$

which must be understood as the displacement of the mass by a small part of the displacement induced by the spring applying the Hooke's law. δ, the adaptative timestep, defines the fraction of the way the node is allowed to move towards the perfect position for the current information. The timestep depends on the local errors of the two nodes (e_i and e_j) and reduces the displacement if the error is important. The timestep is defined by $\delta = c_s \cdot \omega$ where c_s is a tuning constant and $\omega = e_i/(e_i + e_j)$. When a node has computed its new coordinates, it computes its local error $e_i = e_s \cdot \omega + e_i \cdot (1 - \omega)$ where e_s is the *relative error* defined by Eqn. 2. $u(\vec{x}_i - \vec{x}_j)$ gives the direction of the displacement of i and is normalized to 1.

$$e_s = |d_{ij} - \hat{d}_{ij}|/d_{ij}. \tag{2}$$

Eqn. 1 is the core of Vivaldi since it allows nodes to discover their coordinates.

3   Reputation-Based Vivaldi

3.1   A Reputation Model for Embedding Systems

The *reputation* of an entity A is the combination of trusts of all other entities towards A and the *trust* is a subjective expectation that an agent has about another's future behavior based on the history of their encounters [6]. These definitions suggest that reputation is global and objective while trust is local and subjective. The trust is built on the *experiences* the agent observed about A.

In traditional coordinate systems, any node A updates its coordinates based on the coordinates of one of its neighbors and the distance to it. In our new approach, the new coordinates also depend on the reputation of the neighbors. When A updates its coordinates based on measurements with neighbor B, it first contacts B to retrieve its coordinates and reputation. A then computes its coordinates as a function of its own coordinates, B's coordinates and B's reputation. Then, A contacts a special certification agent, the *Reputation Computation Agent* (RCA) to update its own reputation. This RCA is similar to the RCA proposed by [7]. The RCA is used to construct a reliable reputation for any node in the embedded system. For this, we follow the recently proposed approach by Kaafar et al. [8] and introduce new entities in the system: The *surveyors*. A few surveyors are attached to each node in the system. Surveyors are well chosen nodes that perform experiences measurements and trust estimation on other nodes. Next, the RCA computes its own trust to A's surveyors. Finally, the RCA computes the new reputation of A with all these parameters. The RCA introduces scalability issue so that a solution must be found to allow replication of this entity [9].

We now propose a more formal approach to the notions of experience, trust and reputation.

Experience Model. At time t, an experience is an observation of a node A about some behavior of another node B. This observation is evaluated as follows.

$$\xi(A, B, t) = 1 - \frac{\left|\hat{d}(A, B, t) - d(A, B, t)\right|}{\max\left(d(A, B, t), \hat{d}(A, B, t)\right)}. \tag{3}$$

Where $\hat{d}(A, B, t)$ is the estimated distance between A and B and $d(A, B, t)$ is the real distance. This metric is derived from the relative error (Eqn. 2).

The relative error gives information about the accuracy of the predicted distances. The lower the relatives errors are, the accurate the coordinates are. The experience converts the relative error in the bounded interval $[0, 1]$. The experience is maximum for a perfect estimation and decreases with the augmentation of the *prediction error*.

Trust Model. The trust A has in B is an expectation of the future behavior of a node based on the previous experiences A had in B. However, the experience that we defined before depends on external elements and is inherently not absolutely reliable. We use the concept of uncertain probabilities proposed by Jøsang [10] to model this doubt. These uncertain probabilities introduce the concepts of *belief* (*b*), *disbelief* (*d*) and *uncertainty* (*u*). The belief is the probability that the affirmation is true while the disbelief is the probability that this affirmation is false. The uncertainty quantifies the doubt associated to the affirmation. These three concepts together compose an *opinion* which is a tuple $\omega = (b, d, u)$ [11]. Belief, disbelief and uncertainty are linked together by the *belief function additivity* which states that $b + d + u = 1$.

Conceptually, the trust must limit the risk of nodes using multiple identities. It incites therefore nodes to remain in the system for a long time. However, the trust must be reactive enough to adapt to sudden changes in the topology [7]. These requirements can be achieved by using the concept of *trustworthiness*. The trustworthiness $\tau(A, B, t)$ of A in B at time t is an exponentially averaged sum of the experiences [12] multiplied by an ageing factor:

$$\tau(A, B, t) = a(t) \cdot \gamma \cdot \left(\sum_{i=0}^{h} (1 - \gamma)^i \cdot \xi(A, B, t - i) \right). \tag{4}$$

where $a(t)$ is the ageing factor $(a(0) = 0)$, γ is a weighting constant and h is the number of previous experiences that must be taken into account. The exponentially averaged sum of the experiences gives more importance to the most recent experiences [12]. The ageing factor increases with the seniority and limits the trustworthiness of recent nodes (similar to the loss factor proposed in [13]). It is defined as follows:

$$a(t) = c_a + (1 - c_a) \cdot a(t - 1). \tag{5}$$

Where c_a is the age bonus coefficient such that $0 < c_a < 1$ and $a(0) = 0$. c_a controls the gain of the age for the trust computation. The value of c_a is a tradeoff between wisdom and convergence time. A low value of c_a implies a slow convergence to 1, meaning that only old nodes may completely benefit from the experiences. On the contrary, a large value quickly increases the ageing factor to 1 allowing recent nodes to use their entire experience rapidly.

The *untrustworthiness*, $\bar{\tau}(A, B, t)$, is the complement to 1 of the trustworthiness. The *doubt* $\varepsilon(A, B, t)$ A has in B at time t is the variation of the experiences with the time. This variation is estimated with the variance of the last h experiences:

$$\varepsilon(A, B, t) = \sigma \left(\bigcup_{i \in \{0..h\}} \xi(A, B, t - i) \right). \tag{6}$$

The model of uncertain probabilities offers strong perspectives to the reputation in general. The trust $\omega(A, B, t) = (b_B^A(t), d_B^A(t), u_B^A(t))$ the node A has in B at time t has the following bijection with trustworthiness, untrustworthiness and doubt:

$$
\begin{aligned}
b_B^A(t) &= \frac{\tau(A,B,t)}{(\tau(A,B,t)+\bar{\tau}(A,B,t)+\varepsilon(A,B,t))} \\
d_B^A(t) &= \frac{\bar{\tau}(A,B,t)}{(\tau(A,B,t)+\bar{\tau}(A,B,t)+\varepsilon(A,B,t))} \\
u_B^A(t) &= \frac{\varepsilon(A,B,t)}{(\tau(A,B,t)+\bar{\tau}(A,B,t)+\varepsilon(A,B,t))}.
\end{aligned} \tag{7}
$$

Reputation Model. The reputation of an entity at a particular time must be unique and must be a function of the trust that all nodes have in it. However, for scalability reasons, it is impossible to construct a fully-meshed reputation model where each node cooperates with all others to exchange trust information. We therefore propose a *pseudo-reputation* model in which only a few nodes cooperate to determine the reputation.

The uncertain probabilities model proposes two evidential operators [10,11]: *discounting* ($\otimes$) and *consensus* ($\oplus$). The first one can be seen as an operator of transitivity and the second as an operator of averaging. Each node has a set of well-chosen surveyors assigned to it [8]. The surveyors are normal nodes in the system. A surveyor measures the experiences of its assigned nodes. When the reputation of node A has to be updated, the RCA computes its trust in the A's surveyors and combines these trusts with the trust the surveyors have in A. This process is formalized as follows:

$$
\hat{\omega}_A^{RCA} = \bigoplus_{\{H_n \in S_A\}} \tilde{\omega}_{H_n}^{RCA} \otimes \hat{\omega}_A^{H_n}. \tag{8}
$$

Where $\tilde{\omega}_{H_n}^{RCA}$ is the opinion the RCA has in H_n, the nth surveyor of A. In this opinion, the experience is not computed with Eqn. 3 but with Eqn. 9. This particular experience is introduced to avoid the RCA to have to compute its own coordinates. Indeed, if the RCA had coordinates, it would be easy for an attacker to alter the coordinates of the RCA and invalidate the reputation model.

$$
\xi(RCA, H_n, t) = 1 - \frac{\sqrt{\sigma\left(\vec{v}_A^{H_n}(t)/n^2\right)}}{\#\vec{v}_A^{H_n}(t)}. \tag{9}
$$

$\vec{v}_A^{H_n}(t)$ is the variation history. $\#\vec{x}$ is the size of the variation history vector and n is a normalization factor computed by Eqn. 11. The variation history vector is the history at time t of the last h variations of coordinates that the RCA has observed for node A (see Eqn. 10). The intuition behind the division by $\#\vec{v}_A^{H_n}(t)$ is that a large variance in a small set is more abnormal than a similar variance in a large set. The normalization is used to bound the experience within $[0, 1]$.

$$
\vec{v}_A^{H_n}(t) = \langle \|\vec{c}_{t-h} - \vec{c}_{t-h+1}\|, \ldots, \|\vec{c}_{t-1} - \vec{c}_t\| \rangle. \tag{10}
$$

$$n = argmax \left(\bigcup_{\{H_n \in S_A\}} \overrightarrow{v}_A^{H_n}(t) \right). \tag{11}$$

We define the scalar reputation $\hat{\varrho}_A$ of a node A based on the opinion $\hat{\omega}_A^{RCA}$ in the equation 12.

$$\hat{\varrho}_A = \hat{b}_A^{RCA} \cdot (1 - \hat{u}_A^{RCA}). \tag{12}$$

The scalar reputation is the belief in A weighted by the doubt that persists on that affirmation. A receives the scalar reputation as a time-limited ticket. Hence, the RCA is never contacted to retrieve coordinates and does not become a bottleneck [7]. The ticket is digitally signed by the RCA to avoid tampering. More details about the ageing factor and reputation are given in [9].

3.2   Application to Vivaldi

It is possible to improve the robustness of Vivaldi by introducing the notion of reputation in Eqn. 1 of Vivaldi which computes the new coordinates of B based on the knowledge B has in A. This modification is presented in Eqn. 13.

$$\overrightarrow{x}_B = \overrightarrow{x}_B + (\hat{\varrho}_B \cdot \delta) \cdot \left(d_{BA} - \hat{d}_{BA} \right) \cdot u \left(\overrightarrow{x}_B - \overrightarrow{x}_A \right). \tag{13}$$

Vivaldi has been proposed for environments without attackers and works well in that case. The idea is to keep Vivaldi when the neighbor is reliable and to limit the modification of coordinates if the neighbor is not reliable. When the reputation is at its maximum (i.e., $\hat{\varrho}_B = 1$), the modification is the same as traditional Vivaldi. On the contrary, when the reputation is at its worst (i.e., $\hat{\varrho}_B = 0$), the coordinates are not modified.

4   Evaluation

We validate our proposition using the King data set, as performed in the original Vivaldi experimentation [3]. This data set gives a matrix of RTTs between 1740 nodes spread around the world. Our simulator considers 32 neighbors randomly chosen among the entire set of 1740 nodes. The attackers (i.e., the malicious nodes) are fixed at the beginning of the simulation. Attackers reply with random coordinates each time a node asks coordinates. Such an attack is called a *random coordinates attack*. Note that the reputation is protected such that a malicious node cannot modify its own reputation. Only the RCA is able to modify a reputation of the nodes and the RCA is perfectly reliable.

We consider the following proportion of malicious nodes among the entire nodes set: 0% (i.e., there is no attack), 10%, 20%, 50% and 70%. We compare the performance of classic Vivaldi with RVivaldi, as described in Sec. 3.2. The constants used during the simulation are $c_c = 0.25, c_s = 0.25, h = 10, \gamma = 0.5$ and $c_a = 0.01$. The coordinate space is the classic 3-dimensions Euclidean space.

The relative errors (Eqn. 2) are good estimators of the accuracy of the co-ordinates. Fig. 1 shows the cumulative distribution of the relative error of the

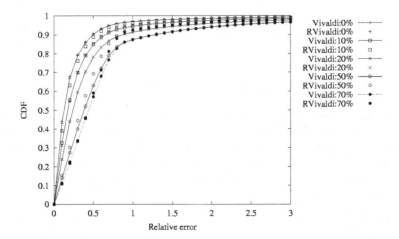

Fig. 1. Random coordinate attack: CDF of relative error at simulation tick = 4000

victims of a random coordinates attack. The vertical axis is the cumulative fraction of nodes and horizontal axis is the value of the relative error. In absence of attackers, RVivaldi does not provide better results than Vivaldi. However, when some malicious nodes are present, RVivaldi outperforms Vivaldi, whatever the relative errors. For example, in presence of 20% of attackers, RVivaldi is as accurate as Vivaldi in presence of only 10% of malicious nodes. RVivaldi mainly outperforms Vivaldi for relative errors between 0.4 and 1.5. Regarding lower or higher relative error, RVivaldi and Vivaldi converge in the same manner. This error can be explained by the error introduced by the coordinate system itself. A more precise evaluation of RVivaldi can be found in [9].

These results confirm that adding reputation to coordinate systems permit to reduce the incidence of attacks on the accuracy of the whole system.

5   Conclusion

Coordinate systems, such as Vivaldi, might be used in various applications where the notion of proximity, expressed as network delay or RTT, is used. However, it has been recently shown that such a system is sensible to attacks. Indeed, a malicious node can lie about its coordinates and, as a consequence, deform the coordinate space. In this paper, we proposed a formal reputation model for coordinate systems. The reputation gives an estimator of the probability a node lies about its coordinates based on the previous experiences with this node.

In addition, we applied this model to Vivaldi and proposed RVivaldi, a reputation adaptation of Vivaldi. We validated RVivaldi using the King data set and showed that adding reputation to Vivaldi improves the accuracy of coordinates in presence of malicious nodes.

In the near future, we aim at validating RVivaldi in a real environment, such as PlanetLab. We further aim at confronting RVivaldi with all the attacks proposed by Kaafar et al. [5]. Moreover, a solution must be proposed to secure the surveyors and the RCA and to avoid it to be a single point of failure.

Acknowledgements

This work was partially supported by the European-founded 034819 OneLab project. Authors would like also to thank Laurent Mathy for his suggestions.

References

1. Francis, P., Jamin, S., Paxson, V., Zhang, L., Gruniewicz, D.F., Jin, Y.: An architecture for a global internet host distance estimator service. In: Proc. IEEE INFOCOM, IEEE Computer Society Press, Los Alamitos (1999)
2. Ng, T.S.E., Zhang, H.: A network positioning system for the internet. In: Proc. USENIX Annual Technical Conference (2004)
3. Dabek, F., Cox, R., Kaashoek, K., Morris, R.: Vivaldi, a decentralized network coordinated system. In: Proc. ACM SIGCOMM, ACM Press, New York (2004)
4. Ledlie, J., Gardner, P., Seltzer, M.: Network coordinates in the wild. In: Proc. Symposium on Networked Systems Design and Implementation (NSDI) (2007)
5. Kaafar, M., Mathy, L., Turletti, T., Dabbous, W.: Virtual networks under attack: Disrupting internet coordinate systems. In: Proc. ACM CoNEXT, ACM Press, New York (2006)
6. Kinateder, M., Rothermel, K.: Architecture and algorithms for a distributed reputation system. In: Proc. 1st Conference on Trust Management (2003)
7. Gupta, M., Judge, P., Ammar, M.: A reputation system for peer-to-peer networks. In: Proc. 13th ACM International Workshop on Network and Operating Systems Support for Digital Audio and Video (NOSSDAV), ACM Press, New York (2003)
8. Kaafar, M., Mathy, L., Barakat, C., Salamatian, K., Turletti, T., Dabbous, W.: Securing internet coordinate embedding systems. In: Proc. ACM SIGCOMM 2008, ACM Press, New York (2008)
9. Saucez, D.: Securing network coordinate systems. Master's thesis, Université Catholique de Louvain (UCL), Belgium (2007)
10. Jøsang, A.: A logic for uncertain probabilities. International Journal of Uncertainty, Fuzziness and Knowledge-Based Systems 9(3), 279–311 (2001)
11. Twigg, A.: A subjective approach to routing in p2p and ad hoc networks. In: Proc. 1st Conference on Trust Management (iTrust) (2003)
12. Yu, B., Singh, M., Sycara, K.: Developing trust in large-scale peer-to-peer systems. In: Proc. 1st IEEE Symposium on Multi-Agent Security and Survivability, IEEE Computer Society Press, Los Alamitos (2004)
13. de Launois, C., Uhlig, S., Bonaventure, O.: Scalable route selection for IPv6 multihomed sites. In: Proc. IFIP Networking (2005)

Source Traffic Characterization for Thin Client Based Office Applications

Barbara Emmert[*], Andreas Binzenhöfer, Daniel Schlosser, and Markus Weiß

University of Würzburg, Institute of Computer Science, Würzburg Germany
[*]emmert@informatik.uni-wuerzburg.de

Abstract. A thin client is a small network computer which is used as a remote screen visualizing the output of software applications running on a central server. To provide a seamless service to thin client users the network connection between the client and the server must be dimensioned properly. In this paper we therefore characterize the traffic generated by different types of thin client users when working with popular office applications like Microsoft Word, Excel, or PowerPoint. We analyze the traffic patterns measured in our testbed environment and thus provide a basis for subsequent research studies as well as for administrators to estimate the amount and the characteristics of user generated traffic.

1 Introduction

There are different ways for a company to provide their employees with the software they need to fulfill their jobs. The most common solutions are to install the applications locally on each client or to provide the software over network file systems. However, both approaches require that every desktop system has enough resources to run the application. An alternative is to run all applications on a central server and merely show the results on thin clients. While this solution is slightly less comfortable for the end-user, it reduces the initial expenditures as well as the current energy and maintenance costs. As a side-effect it also becomes easier for an administrator to manage the software suite as well as to install updates and patches. For the same reasons, the concept of application service providing (ASP) has become popular, especially among small and mid sized organizations. One of the services an ASP offers to its customers is to host desktop-type applications on a server farm and to provide access, administration, and support.

Originally, the thin client architecture was designed for local area networks (LAN). However, an increasing number of clients is connected via wide area networks (WAN) or over leased lines. The problem of this development is that the network connection (possibly shared by all clients) can easily become a bottleneck and affect the service quality experienced by the end-user. In order to properly dimension the company network and the lines rented for home office workers, the traffic generated by a thin client user must be well understood.

---

[*] Corresponding author.

A. Pras and M. van Sinderen (Eds.): EUNICE 2007, LNCS 4606, pp. 86–94, 2007.

In this paper we therefore characterize the traffic flow between a typical thin client and the widely used Citrix Presentation Server 4.0 [1]. This traffic depends not only on the implementation of the underlying ICA protocol, but also on the application in use and the behavior of the end-user. On that account we measure the traffic generated by different types of users working with Word, Excel, and PowerPoint, the most popular applications from the Microsoft Office suite. We will compare different scenarios and applications in terms of important characteristics like used packet sizes, bandwidth consumption, and time between packets. Thereby we differentiate between the traffic produced by the server and the traffic produced by the thin client. The results from our measurements are useful for companies to properly dimension their networks according to the expected number of clients as well as for researchers conducting analytical or simulative studies in a thin client environment.

The remainder of this paper is organized as follows. Section 2 gives a brief overview of related work. The measurement setup as well as the measurement methodology are explained in Section 3. We discuss the different scenarios, the results, and their implications in Section 4, Section 5 finally concludes this work.

2 Related Work

As simulation is an important tool for networking research, it is vital to generate realistic traffic streams. Due to the overwhelming dominance of web traffic in contemporary WANs, most source traffic models focus on this fraction of the utilized bandwidth. So does the stochastic source traffic model for HTTP traffic proposed by Cao et al. [2]. The authors analyzed packet traces from two links connecting medium sized organizations to the Internet. A more general approach has been proposed by Staehle et al. [3], who established a source traffic model for realistic wireless simulations. For this purpose, they introduced a single user traffic model which considers Email, HTTP, FTP, and WAP traffic.

The number of ASPs hosting office applications for remote users is growing, but the percentage of bandwidth consumed by this type of service remains negligible. Therefore, little work has been dedicated to analyzing the characteristics of traffic caused by thin client based applications. One of the few studies in this area has been performed by the Tolly Group [4] who evaluated the usability of Microsoft PowerPoint via WAN. They investigated the consumed bandwidth and completion time of a common PowerPoint operation executed on a machine running Citrix MetaFrame XP client software accessing a server hosting the corresponding Presentation Server. They report "on machine" experience for high bandwidth links like Fast Ethernet, Ethernet, or WLAN and up to twice as long completion times for slower links. Tolia et al. [5] evaluated VNC performance, focusing on the operation response times for image processing, presentation creating, and text processing. Their findings show that highly interactive applications are more sensitive to a higher network round trip time than simpler applications. More general measurements are reported by Lai and Nieh [6], who evaluated the performance of thin client computing in a WAN.

For their work, they used both measurements in the Internet2 and simulations in a testbed. One of the investigated characteristics was the completion time of typical office tasks like typing, scrolling, or image downloading. To analyze the difference between the considered platforms, they compared the amount of data transferred before the completion of each test, the required bandwidth, and the test duration. The fact that the typing task was completed faster, and required less bandwidth than scrolling already gave a first insight into the structure of traffic caused by office applications. In this work, however, we intend to specify the characteristics of the emerging traffic in more detail. In particular, we distinguish between the client and the server side, different user behavior as well as different office applications.

3   Measurement Setup and Methodology

In order to measure and characterize the traffic of thin client applications, we set up a typical thin client environment as depicted in Figure 1. It consists of a

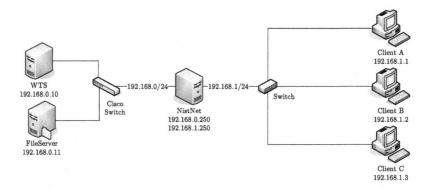

Fig. 1. Overview of the measurement setup

server farm which is accessed by three clients and a network emulator running NistNet [7], which enables us to alter delay, jitter, and packet loss of the end-to-end connection. The Windows Terminal Server as well as the corresponding file server are Intel Xenon 3.4 Ghz machines with 3.5 GB RAM running Windows 2003 Server in the standard edition with service pack 1. The clients are Pentium III 2.6 Ghz machines with 1 GB RAM running on Windows XP Professional with service pack 2. The Windows Terminal server hosts the entire Microsoft Office 2003 product family and runs Citrix Presentation Server 4.0 to make these applications available for remote users. The clients use version 9.237 of the ICA client to access the applications hosted on the server. This setup enables us to generate and measure thin client caused traffic in a controlled environment.

Our emulation experiments are set up as follows. At first the client opens a Citrix session and starts the corresponding application. It then performs different tasks which are typical for office users. To automate this procedure, we used AutoHotkey [8], which is able to carry out keystrokes as well as mouse movements and clicks according to a simple macro language. This way, we are, e.g., able to emulate different typing speeds in Word or the insertion of pictures into a PowerPoint slide. To capture the corresponding processes on network level, we recorded packet traces using Windump [9] on both the client and the server machines, which could then be analyzed offline.

4   Measurements and Results

The traffic generated by a thin-client on packet level depends on both the application and the behavior of the user. Intuitively, the activity of the user directly corresponds to the amount of consumed network bandwidth. To verify this assumption, we will therefore regard different office applications and characterize the source traffic created by different types of users of which we distinguish light, normal, and power users, in the following.

4.1   Analysis of Typical Word Tasks

thin client traffic, we emulated typical tasks performed by a Microsoft Word user like typing, scrolling, or selecting menu entries. During the typing test, the user continuously types text and thereby corrects some misspelled words. He then scrolls the document using the scroll bar and selects some entries from the menu bar. Figure 2(a) confirms that the different tasks require different amounts of bandwidth on network level. Thereby scrolling consumes the most bandwidth as large parts of the screen need to be refreshed.

More interesting observations, however, can be made when looking at the sizes of the packets which were sent by the client during the emulation as shown in Figure 2(b). Almost all packets sent by the client are either 40 byte TCP

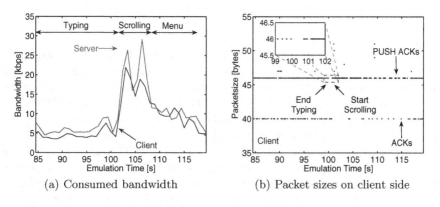

(a) Consumed bandwidth   (b) Packet sizes on client side

Fig. 2. Characteristics of typical Word tasks

acknowledgments or 46 byte TCP push acknowledgments. That is, the Citrix client encodes all user input using 6 byte payload and setting the TCP push flag to enforce the immediate delivery of the data. Thereby, instead of sending packets of larger size, the ICA protocol prefers to reduce the time between packets in times of higher bandwidth utilization. This can nicely be seen in the zoomed area in Figure 2(b), which shows that the time between two sent packets is significantly smaller when scrolling than while typing. Thus, in the design of the ICA protocol, responsiveness seems to have played a more important role than overhead.

4.2   Impact of the User Behavior

Next, we analyzed the traffic caused by different types of typing users. The results shown in Figure 3 were obtained by emulating a user who types the beginning of Orwell's "War of the Worlds" for 10 minutes. We considered typing speeds of 100, 250, and 400 characters per minute (cpm) as to be typical for light, normal, and power users respectively. For comparison purposes, we also include results obtained for 500 cpm.

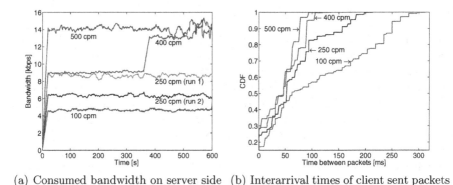

(a) Consumed bandwidth on server side   (b) Interarrival times of client sent packets

Fig. 3. Traffic characteristics varying with typing speed

When different types of users were emulated, the bandwidth consumed by the client varies between 2 and 7 kbps. In Figure 3(a) we show 20 s moving averages of the bandwidth consumed by the server for the same experiment. The abrupt rise in the curve representing the power user (400 cpm) in Figure 3(a) is illustrating our observations during the measurements: In some cases, the consumed bandwidth suddenly grew by a significant amount, but remained constant before and after this event. As this increase is too fast for being TCP triggered, we assume that an ICA-intern QoS mechanism is responsible for it. This appears also to be the reason, why the obtained mean values for a normal user (250 cpm) differ by more than 2 kbps for two different experiments (run 1 and run 2). However, the total of our measurements showed, that besides the mentioned increases, which did not occur on client side, a typing user consumes a nearly constant amount between 4 and 15 kbps of network bandwidth depending on the typing speed.

The comparison of interarrival times of client sent packets in Figure 3(b) shows results similar to the observations described in the last section: The cumulative density functions (CDFs) illustrate that the client increases the bandwidth by sending out packets faster in the case of a more active user. The server sent larger packets, while the size of most client packets was 46 byte. Thus the Citrix client adapts to the user behavior by varying the time between two packets instead of the packet size.

4.3   Comparison of Different Office Applications

Figure 4 visualizes the impact of the application type on the network traffic. For this experiment we compared the emulations of users searching and selecting menu entries under Word, inserting text, pictures as well as looking at animations under PowerPoint and selecting fields in an Excel data sheet.

First, we compared the consumed server side bandwidth. Again, the bandwidth consumed by the client was smaller and was only 2 kbps in the case where the animation was displayed. Note that in Figure 4(a) we do not show the bandwidth consumed for the insertion of pictures in a PowerPoint presentation, as the used files were roughly of size 2 MB. The amount of consumed bandwidth was thus significantly larger than for all other tasks. We were however surprised, that the compared 20 s moving averages for the Excel test and for Word menu operations were significantly higher than for displaying animations, which lay roughly in the range of inserting text in a presentation. The variations in the bandwidth of the latter test may arise from the necessary creation of new slides, a task which requires bandwidth intense mouse movements. All in all, we saw again that while the consumed bandwidth differs quite strongly between the applications, it is nearly constant for each single task.

As in the earlier described cases, the size of packets sent by the client is almost constant. The size of the server sent packets, however, differs strongly

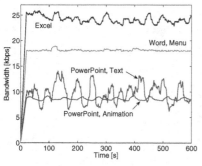

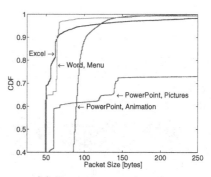

(a) Bandwidth consumed on server side   (b) Server sent packet sizes

Fig. 4. Traffic characteristics varying with applications

between the measurements (see Figure 4(b)). Note that for the case of highly interactive mouse operations (Excel and Word menu), the size of more than 50 % of all packets is only 40 byte, i.e. those packets are acknowledgments. Our measurements showed that, similar to the typing tests analyzed earlier, the responsiveness seems to be improved by sending packets faster. This does however not hold for the case of animations and pictures under PowerPoint, where the bandwidth increase is done by sending larger packets. Another interesting fact is illustrated by the CDF in Figure 4(b) representing the insertion of pictures in a presentation: While all inserted pictures were stored on the client, the large packet sizes observed during the experiment indicate, that for presentation purposes the picture files still have to be transferred to the server.

4.4 Characterization of Server Side Traffic

Our last experiment was dedicated to a deeper investigation of the server sent packet sizes. For this purpose, we analyzed traces collected during the insertion of pictures and the visualization of different animations under PowerPoint. A shorter and a longer animation were compared and the influence of the maximum transfer unit set at the server were investigated.

Figure 5(a) visualizes the autocorrelation of server sent packet sizes for a lag up to 800. Apart from two spikes in the case of Animation 1 and one spike in the case of Animation 2, the autocorrelation is not significant, but fluctuating. This indicates, that the traffic caused by animations is not bursty, but that quite often an acknowledgment packet seems to be transferred just after a larger data packet. The spikes correspond to the duration of the animation which was shorter in the first case.

The comparison of the two experiments of picture insertion reveals that, while the autocorrelation is fluctuating quite strongly in the case where the server MTU was set to 1394 byte, this is not the case, if the MTU is set to 1500 byte. Both autocorrelations are not significant any more after a given time which corresponds to the transmission of a picture. The reasons for the different shapes and slopes of the curves become apparent in Figure 5(b), where we show for each

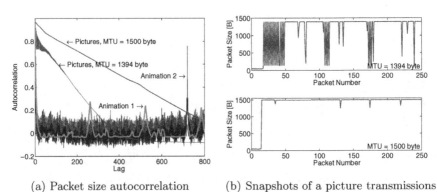

(a) Packet size autocorrelation   (b) Snapshots of a picture transmissions

Fig. 5. Server sent packet size characteristics for different PowerPoint tasks

measurement a snapshot of 250 subsequent sent packets. In both cases, we chose the begin of a picture transmission. Observe that for the case, where the smaller maximum packet size is chosen, very often a small packet of around 200 byte is following a large packet of 1394 byte. This is however, not the case if the MTU is set to 1500 byte: Under this configuration, the most common packet size is corresponding to the maximal feasible value. Furthermore, smaller packet sizes are only used for acknowledgments which gives the autocorrelation a higher value than in the first case. These results indicate that the Presentation Server tries to send packets of 1500 byte in both cases, which are defragmented by the operation system under the first configuration. Thus, if large pictures or files have to be transmitted, the parameter settings of the operating system and the ICA protocol have to be chosen and adapted with care to avoid unnecessary transmission delays and bandwidth consumption.

5   Conclusion

Despite their growing popularity, little is known about the characteristics of traffic generated by thin client based applications. In this paper, we therefore analyzed different office applications, published by Citrix Presentation Server 4.0 and accessed by thin clients, by measurements on the network layer. During our experiments, we found that the user input, like keystrokes or mouse movements, is mainly encoded with a payload of 6 byte. Thereby higher bandwidth rates are mainly achieved by decreasing the time between two packets while keeping the size of the packets constant. This indicates that in the design of the underlying ICA protocol, responsiveness played a more important role than efficient bandwidth usage. We found moreover, that keyboard input causes less traffic than mouse movements or the transfer of large files, but that PowerPoint animations consume comparatively small amounts of bandwidth. Our measurements showed furthermore, that except for the transmissions of large files, the autocorrelation of the packet sizes is rather small, which indicates that the considered thin client traffic is not bursty.

The results presented in this work can be used by system administrators to understand ICA traffic and help in network bandwidth dimensioning when updating existing or designing new thin client architectures. However, special care should be taken when setting the size of the maximum transfer unit at the server: values smaller than 1500 byte (likely to be used in VPNs) may possibly increase bandwidth consumptions and transmission delays of large files, thus decreasing the user perceived quality of experience.

Acknowledgments

The authors would like to thank Björn Boder for the insightful discussions as well as for providing the hardware necessary to conduct the studies.

References

1. Citrix Systems, Inc., http://www.citrix.com
2. Cao, J., Cleveland, W., Gao, Y., Jeffay, K., Smith, F., Weigle, M.: Stochastic Models for Generating Synthetic HTTP Source Traffic. In: IEEE INFOCOM 2004, Hong Kong, China, March 2004, IEEE Computer Society Press, Los Alamitos (2004)
3. Staehle, D., Leibnitz, K., Tran-Gia, P.: Source Traffic Modeling of Wireless Applications. Technical Report 261, University of Würzburg, Institute of Computer Science (June 2000)
4. The Tolly Group: Citrix Systems, Inc. MetaFrame XP Presentation Server Windows-based Application Access Performance and Functionality (2003)
5. Tolia, N., Andersen, D.G., Satyanarayanan, M.: Quantifying Interactive User Experience on Thin Clients. IEEE Computer Society Press Computer 39(3) (2006)
6. Lai, A.M., Nieh, J.: On the Performance of Wide-Area Thin-Client Computing. ACM Transactions on Computer Systems 24(2) (2006)
7. Carson, M., Santay, D.: NistNet: a Linux-based network emulation tool. SIGCOMM Computer Communication Review 33(3) (2003)
8. AutoHotkey. http://www.autohotkey.com/
9. WinPcap. http://www.winpcap.org/

Legal Compliance in Commercial Service Provisioning Across Administrative Domains

Martin Waldburger[1] and Burkhard Stiller[1,2]

[1] University of Zürich, Department of Informatics (IFI), CH–8050 Zürich
[2] ETH Zürich, Computer Engineering and Networks Lab (TIK), CH–8092 Zürich
{waldburger, stiller}@ifi.uzh.ch

Abstract. Internet design principles do not focus on commercial service provisioning. Hence, support mechanisms need to be implemented in order to ensure that value added services can be offered in a competitive context. Commercial product offerings base on contractual agreements concluded between service providers and service customers. Contracts need to reflect business-driven requirements originating from involved contract parties, while they are invariably required to respect those regulations imposed by commerce law. Legal compliance, thus, determines the available range of applicable contractual terms—irrespective of whether such a contract governs commercial value added services in the Internet or not. Legal determinations are valid in a limited geographical area. The Internet, however, lacks a distinct notion of location. Consequently, technical means to overcome this fundamental design gap are investigated, in order to ensure that legally compliant contracts can be concluded.

1 Introduction and Motivation

In order to offer commercial electronic value added services in the Internet respective support mechanisms have to be in place. The minimum range of required mechanisms is determined by those requirements put in order by commerce law. Even though these legislations have a long tradition of being part in civil code determinations, they originally do not consider specifics of electronic service provisioning. Hence, potential adaptations with regard to an application to electronic service provisioning need to be included. Such adaptations comprise mechanisms for Authentication, Authorization, Accounting, Auditing, and Charging (A4C) [8,6] as these elements document the timely course of actions in electronic business transactions.

In the Internet, which is organized as a network of networks, complexity in commercial electronic service provisioning appears to be increased, since trade partners are decoupled from shared room and time experience. In contrast to certain non-electronic business transactions, where physical presence of trade partners might be a sufficient replacement for procedures that explicitly ensure partner identification (authentication) and that assess their respective entitlements (authorization), authentication and authorization are typically mandatory elements in electronic business transactions.

A4C reflects those functional elements typically required for commercial electronic transactions to be compliant with external or self-imposed regulations. This considers

A. Pras and M. van Sinderen (Eds.): EUNICE 2007, LNCS 4606, pp. 95–102, 2007.

the direct understanding of legal compliance. However, legislations traditionally are unaware of electronic commerce. Driven by technological dependencies originating from the TCP/IP-based Internet protocol stack and the Internet's organizational composition from various administrative domains, both, the commercial transaction as such and A4C support mechanisms need to be legally compliant, thus, resulting in an integrated viewpoint on legal compliance.

In this context, different challenging issues arise, out of which the lacking notion of territoriality in the Internet reveals a design gap so fundamental in nature that it potentially menaces legal compliance of commercial electronic service provisioning *per se*. Commercial value added services base on contracts that are concluded between service providers and service consumers. Contracts are subject to commerce law regulations, whereas these regulations are valid in a geographically limited area, typically within a territory. The Internet, however, lacks a notion of geographical location. Thus, technical means for automated contract conclusion in the Internet have to be investigated, designed, implemented, and evaluated. These mechanisms require legal procedures for international contract formation to be followed and the Internet to be equipped by a notion of location.

Accordingly, the remainder of this paper is structured as follows: Section 2 provides the key legal and technical background relevant for this work. Legal aspects of interest include careful inspection of conflicting law systems and the process of forming contracts in an international context, thus, in a situation where service provider and service customer potentially are located in another legal domain, *i.e.* another territory. Technical aspects of interest embrace the multi-domain, but extra-territorial nature of the Internet. Based on this background information, the research problem to be addressed is determined in Section 3, whereas the initial approach to a solution and the current status of work are presented in Section 4.

2   Legal and Technical Background

For a complete understanding of those consequences implied by territorial nature of (western) law and by the extra-territorial constitution of the Internet, an in-depth investigation into the respective domains of law systems and the organization of the Internet is required. Hence, this section addresses fundamental background information on legal and Internet design principles for contracts that need to be concluded in a global context. In particular, differing notions of domains for regulations (territories) and in the Internet (administrative domains) are outlined. These insights given provide the key arguments to state the research problem to be solved (*cf.* Section 3).

2.1   Contract Formation Process in an International Context

Contracts constitute the central element in legal compliance considerations with regard to commercial value added service provisioning. Since the Internet is a global infrastructure, contractual agreements potentially have to be concluded across territorial borders. Law systems of different countries are not fully compatible (*cf.* Section 2.2) so that contractual parties might be required to choose the respective applicable legal system or that arbitration becomes necessary.

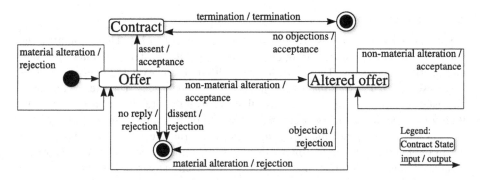

Fig. 1. Contract Formation Finite State Machine Compliant with the United Nations Convention on Contracts for the International Sale of Goods (CISG, [11])

Figure 1 models the process of contract formation for agreements that are governed by the United Nations convention on Contracts for the International Sale of Goods (CISG, [11]). CISG is the most prominent example in law for international contract formation. Depending on the actual situation, other legal determinations need to be considered, *e.g.*, bilateral agreements governing commerce law between two nations.

The depicted automaton visualizes different available possibilities for the so-called offerer (sender of a proposed agreement, called offer) and offeree (the receiver of an offer, an altered or a counter-offer, respectively) in order to consent or dissent on a contract. It includes details on forming a contract, whereas it abstracts from the applicable specifics of contract termination. Figure 1 includes two distinct end states, one for a terminated contract and one for a contract wich cannot be concluded. This separation is important for legal reasons as a terminated contract might imply liability claims.

Upon receipt of an offer, the offeree has two basic choices available. The offeree can either assent or dissent. Assent results in acceptance of the offer, whereas dissent results in rejection of the offer. Assent renders an offer into a contract. Assent subsumes the cases where the offeree assents fully without any modifications to the offer. If the offeree alters the original offer in non-material aspects, the offer is still accepted and becomes automatically effective, unless the offerer explicitly objects. Similarly, dissent subsumes the cases where an offer is ignored until it expires or where the offeree changes the original offer in material aspects. The automaton depicted in Figure 1 does not explicitly model timely behavior, such as that every offer is equipped by a validity time, whereas it includes specifically material alterations to an offer.

Material alterations are determined as contractual terms related to price, payment, quality and quantity of the goods, place and time of delivery, liability determinations, and settlement of disputes [11]. A materially altered offer is automatically rejected and the original order is replaced by the new counter-offer. In Figure 1, this is reflected by returning to the respective initial state of an offer. In contrast to a non-materially altered offer, the counter-offer does not automatically become effective, but requires explicit assent by the new offeree (the former offerer).

2.2 Conflicts of Laws

Seven major legal traditions are identified and presented in [1]. These comprise the chthonic (customary), several religiously inspired and the western (civil law and common law) legal systems. They emerged from different contexts and regions, whereas they mixed partially over time or exist in parallel in some places. Their respective characteristics conflict in several aspects so that full integration is hardly achievable—be it only for specific sub-areas of commerce law. Incompatibilities prevail in traditional cases as much as they become apparent, when considering electronic service provisioning in the Internet. Due to the Internet's global reach the chance for situations, where legal traditions collide in an incompatible way, is even increased. It is the concern of the so-called conflicts of laws, also referred to as private international law, to decide on the question what jurisdiction applies in a specific case.

[1] concludes as "The answer would appear to be that there is no such universalizable core. This is good news for the sustainability of the major, complex, legal traditions of the world." Accordingly and as a matter of last resort, commercial electronic service provision might be declined at all under unresolvable conditions. The approach of roman law which separated into two branches (ius civile applicable to Romans and ius gentium applicable to non-romans) is, however, by no means a solution to conflicts of laws in the Internet. Simply ignoring such conflicts is not feasible in a global context. It would only be feasible, if there was a globally accepted, specific Internet law that could be separated from existing legal systems.

Chances for such an Internet law that is globally accepted are assessed as being low, since as it would collide with national sovereignty. On the other hand, United Nations law on international trade of goods as modeled in Figure 1 is one effort to overcome incompatibilties, whereas it reflects those principles of western commerce law most directly. This is of high relevance since territoriality is not an accepted prinicple in every legal system. Territoriality, however, is a fundamental principle for commerce law in western law systems as legal institutions are recognized in western law as state authorities [1].

Overall, the potential of unresolvable conflicts of laws is fully acknowledged. It is valued as a general open issue in the legal domain that this work needs to be fully aware of. However, it is not the task of this work to determine a solution to it in the most general way. In contrast, this work seeks for a technical solution to conclude legally compliant contracts in the Internet. This solution needs to be based on established legal principles of conflicts of laws. It, thus, aims to implement these principles technically, but it does not seek to change underlying legal principles.

2.3 Internet Organization

Internet design principles, in terms of protocols in use and its organizational composition, as well as dynamics in Internet routing mechanisms determine the key technical background to be investigated. The first area reflects the extra-territorial nature of the Internet, being composed from various administrative domains, but lacking any geographically bound addressing elements. The second area characterizes mechanisms applied in laying out a communications path through intermediate systems from any end system to another.

The Internet is organized as a network of networks. Each of them determines an administrative domain with its own routing policy, whereas actual internal routing details remain undiscovered by others. Traditionally, such a domain is termed autonomous system (AS) [10], identified by a unique number (AS number, ASN). Since ASNs are scarce, it is possible that smaller domains receive a private ASN not visible to all other ASes [4].

Within an AS, the same intra-AS routing protocol (also referred to as Interior Gateway Protocol, IGP) is used whereas inter-AS protocols (Exterior Gateway Protocol, EGP, [10]) regulate routing between border routers of different ASes. The term AS evolved over time from its original perception as a set of systems that make use of the same IGP towards the wider understanding of an administrative domain [2,4]. Routing in this context refers to network routing on layer 3, but it sometimes subsumes in a wider understanding also layer 2 switching, which establishes point-to-point connectivity. When a packet needs to be sent from one end system (ES) [2] to another, routing mechanisms lay out the way the packet takes on its journey through intermediate systems (IS) [2] in terms of routers and switches.

In case a (two-party) contract for a commercial value added service shall be concluded, contractual parties are represented by one ES each. Accordingly, contractual parties are each member of an AS. This implies that contractual parties are identifiable by means of an IP address assigned to the respective ES. Accordingly, ASes are identifiable by the respective ASN a given IP address belongs to. However, the respective territory, or any dependable information on a party's (*i.e.* the respective ES's) geographical location cannot be determined from knowing about a party's AS. Nor is it possible to establish a clear relation between ASes and territories. Contractual parties can either belong to the same AS or to different ASes. Equally, they can reside in the same or different territories. ASes in turn can be fully contained within one territory or they can span multiple (two or more) territories. Moreover, routing mechanisms, influence legal determinations to be considered as conveyed data passes one or several territories. The latter is assumed to take place primarily in cases where contractual parties reside in distant locations, but it can also happen in case parties are associated with the same AS. Routing, thus, shows a high impact on geographical and territorial issues.

Ambiguity in relating ASes to territories constitutes the very essence of the Internet's extra-territorial nature. This design principle collides directly with a regulation's validity that is bound to a geographically limited area. Therefore, legal compliance for contracts in the Internet cannot be accomplished without a mechanism that allows for a reliable mapping of ASes to territories, rendering the Internet into a location-aware infrastructure. This allows to address the problem whether contractual parties can conclude an agreement under given circumstances.

3   Problem Statement

Commercial offerings of value added services in the Internet base on contractual agreements. Applicable contractual terms are expressed in Service Level Agreements (SLA) and technically refined by individual metrics (Service Level Objectives, SLO), whereas a Service Level Specification (SLS) is perceived as a technically interpreted SLA with its SLOs for a given contract [13]. In accordance with those arguments outlined with respect to legal compliance in an international context (*cf.* Sections 2.1 and 2.2) and with respect to administrative and legal domains (*cf.* Section 2.3), two problems are determined as follows:

I) For given parties (in terms of legal entities) and a given electronic service to be provided, a decision has to be taken, if at all and under which governing law a contract can be concluded.
II) Once a contract was agreed upon, the service provision itself needs to be legally compliant with the governing law in question.

Legal compliance in relation to problem I refers to commerce law requirements on concluding contracts and in particular to private international law (conflicts of laws). Legal compliance in relation to problem II refers accordingly to compliance with negotiated contractual terms as characterized by SLS conditions. In order to conduct automated compliance checks on both, problems I and II, two distinct prerequisites are identified:

1) A mapping mechanism from AS to territories is needed.
2) Guaranteed associations between contractual partners need to be taken.

Mapping from AS to territory (or potentially territories) allows contractual parties that are located in an AS (the same AS or different ASes) to be assigned to legal domains. If contractual parties are not bound to a specific location, *i.e.* they are mobile, such a mapping relation needs to deal with dynamics in a flexible manner. Mobility increases additionally the complexity in attributing unambiguously contractual parties to geographical locations.

While prerequisite 1 focuses primarily on the mutual end points of an electronic service provided, prerequisite 2 considers particularly the conveyance of data in between. Due to dynamic routing, no guarantees of persistent associations can be assumed [9]. Figure 2 shows a simplified arrangement of two contractual parties A and B, both located in the same legal domain (LD), where exchanged packets can be routed along one of two possible paths. The association denoted by a dotted line passes another legal domain, where different, potentially conflicting, legal determinations exist. Therefore, ways in routing protocols and behavior need to be found that produce deterministic and reliable expectations on associations, while ensuring not to interfere with the robustness of routing mechanisms. This simplified example visualizes that legal and technical viewpoints are not easily integrated, but require a careful inspection of different scenarios covering the various configurations possible to lay out ESes and ISes, ASes and LDs, and the respective associations.

Fig. 2. Example Associations Between Contractual Partners A and B (LD =Legal Domain)

4 Solution Approach

A technical solution to those problems and prerequisites outlined implies a wide range of activities in different fields to be undertaken. These activities embrace typically each the according set of subactivities, in particular exploration and analysis of existing work, design of a solution, implementation, and evaluation. Overall work status is driven by current exploration and partly design activities which will build the solid basis for upcoming implementation and evaluation phases. Detailed work status information for problems I and II and for prerequisites 1 and 2 is given subsequently.

Problem I is currently in states exploration and analysis of related work as well as design of a solution. An in-depth examination of integration options for the major legal traditions in the world was undertaken based on the comprehensive analysis in [1]. Next steps in this context include careful inspection of conflicts of laws (private international law) processes. Rules of so-called choice of law are of particular interest. Choice of law allows contractual parties to select for an agreement to be concluded what (national) law is applied to the agreement. This includes exemplarily what procedures to follow and what court to call in case of disputes. A comprehensive survey on international agreements, such as the United Nations determinations on contracts for the international sale of goods [11], started recently. This study aims at formalized rules determining under which circumstances contractual parties can use choice of law.

Based on those generalized rules determined in exploration and analysis phase, solution design with regard to problem I forsees the altered contract formation process as visualized in Figure 3. It extends the standard contract formation process (*cf.* Figure 1) by an automated compliance check which is performed after an offer was issued. This compliance check addresses problem I as it answers whether a contract under given terms of an offer can be concluded and what law (choice of law principle) governs the agreement. Successful compliance checks transform an initial offer into a so-called lawful offer. Unsuccessful checks result in non-compliance, which imlies that a contract cannot be concluded. Whenever material alterations are made to a lawful offer or to an altered offer, resulting in rejection and a counter-offer, a new successful compliance check is required in order to render the counter-offer into lawful state.

Similar to problem I, problem II is in states exploration and analysis of related work as well as design of a solution. In order to outline the key characteristics for legal compliance in specific application fields, the domain of mobile grid applications was

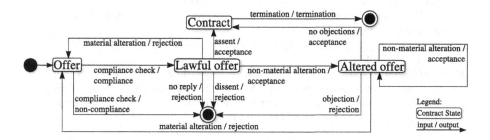

Fig. 3. Altered Contract Formation Finite State Machine

investigated initially [12] and a comprehensive follow-up study is currently conducted. This study focuses on the relevant set of European regulations for commercial value added services, namely policies governing electronic commerce, consumer protection, copyright and related rights, cybercrime, and data protection. Solution design with regard to problem II applies a second type of automated compliance checks. These checks show typical characteristics of auditing tasks. Legal compliance checks are conducted by means of automated SLA compliance checks for regulations-specific metrics [3].

Prerequisites 1 and 2 are currently in exploration and analysis of related work state. For prerequisite 1, investigations on promising approaches are ongoing. This includes mechanisms to retrieve location information from the TCP/IP protocol stack (*e.g.*, derived from latency measurements based on Traceroute [7] or by leveraging a location-verified care-of address as used in mobile IP) or from technical equipment (*e.g.*, by means of certificates provided by a network operator). Similarly, the selection process of candidates to provide the basic mechanisms for a solution to prerequisite 2 started recently. Based on studies on route stability in the Internet [9], Multi Protocol Label Switching (MPLS, [5]) is investigated as a means for laying out a signaled association between contractual partners.

References

1. Glenn, H.P.: Legal Traditions of the World: Sustainable Diversity in Law, 2nd edn., pp. 1–432. Oxford University Press, Oxford (2004)
2. Hares, S., Katz, D.: Administrative Domains and Routing Domains. A Model for Routing in the Internet RFC 1136, pp. 1–10 (December 1989)
3. Hasan, H., Stiller, B.: A Generic Model and Architecture for Automated Auditing. In: Schönwälder, J., Serrat, J. (eds.) DSOM 2005. LNCS, vol. 3775, pp. 121–129. Springer, Heidelberg (2005)
4. Hawkinson, J., Bates, T.: Guidelines for Creation, Selection, and Registration of an Autonomous System (AS). RFC 1930, pp. 1–10 (March 1996)
5. IETF MPLS working group: Multiprotocol Label Switching (MPLS) (March 2006), http://www.ietf.org/html.charters/mpls-charter.html
6. Karsten, M., Schmitt, J., Stiller, B., Wolf, L.: Charging for Packet-switched Network Communication – Motivation and Overview. Computer Communications 23(3), 290–302 (2000)
7. Malkin, G.: Traceroute Using an IP Option. RFC 1393, pp. 1–7 (October 1993)
8. Morariu, C., Waldburger, M., Stiller, B.: An Integrated Accounting and Charging Architecture for Mobile Grids. In: Third International Workshop on Networks for Grid Applications (GridNets 2006), San Jose (CA), USA, pp. 1–10 (October 2006)
9. Paxson, V.: End-to-end Routing Behavior in the Internet. ACM SIGCOMM Computer Communication Review 36(5), 41–56 (2006)
10. Rosen, E.C., Beranek, B.: Newman Inc: Exterior Gateway Protocol (EGP). RFC 827, pp. 1–44 (October 1982)
11. United Nations Commission on International Trade Law (UNCITRAL): United Nations Convention on Contracts for the International Sale of Goods (CISG), pp. 1–47 (April 1980)
12. Waldburger, M., Stiller, B.: Regulatory Issues for Mobile Grid Computing in the European Union. In: 17th European Regional ITS Conference, pp. 1–9 (August 2006)
13. Westerinen, A., et al.: Terminology for Policy-Based Management. RFC 3198, pp. 1–21 (November 2001)

Measurement of the SIP Parsing Performance in the SIP Express Router

Stephan Wanke[1], Michael Scharf[1], Sebastian Kiesel[1], and Stefan Wahl[2]

[1] Institute of Communication Networks and Computer Engineering (IKR),
University of Stuttgart, Germany
[2] Alcatel-Lucent Deutschland AG, Research & Innovation Germany

Abstract. Future telephony and multimedia systems will use the Session Initiation Protocol (SIP) for signaling purposes. SIP is a text-based protocol that imposes challenges for an efficient message processing. The ability of SIP entities to process SIP messages quickly is crucial for the performance of these networks, which often have strict timing requirements, e. g., to keep the call setup delays small.

This paper studies the performance of SIP message processing in SIP proxies, focusing mainly on the impact of message parsing. We perform a detailed delay analysis for the widely used SIP Express Router (SER). Our measurements show that message parsing actually contributes significantly to a SIP proxy's processing efforts, and therefore confirm other existing studies. However, our results also show that the overall delay in high-performance SIP proxies is stronger affected by other factors, in particular the operating system.

1 Introduction

The Session Initiation Protocol (SIP) is the de facto standard for session signaling in IP-based telephony and multimedia systems, such as the 3GPP IP Multimedia Subsystem (IMS) [1] or ETSI TISPAN. In these systems, many entities are involved in call control and many SIP messages are exchanged for time-critical signaling flows like call setups. Signaling latencies depend on a variety of factors, including both transport and processing delays. This is why the ability of SIP entities to process SIP messages effectively is crucial for the overall network performance. SIP is a text-based protocol. Therefore, SIP entities have to parse text messages, which is reported in literature to consume significant amounts of processing time [2]. This has also fostered proposals to use alternative encoding formats for session signaling; a recent example is, e. g., [3].

The purpose of this paper is to understand the performance impact of SIP message parsing. In spite of many research efforts on SIP signaling, surprisingly little work has been published on the performance of SIP entities. We report detailed performance measurements that have been obtained from the SIP Express Router, which is a widely used high-performance SIP proxy. They confirm that SIP parsing indeed consumes significant processing power. However, our results

A. Pras and M. van Sinderen (Eds.): EUNICE 2007, LNCS 4606, pp. 103–110, 2007.

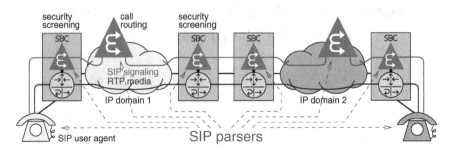

Fig. 1. SIP protocol entities in a carrier-grade VoIP network (simplified)

also reveal that other factors such as the operating system have a very significant impact, too. These effects are hardly addressed in other published studies.

The remainder of this paper is structured as follows: Section 2 gives an overview of SIP performance in signaling systems and also reviews related work. In Section 3, the testbed for our measurements is presented. In Section 4, we report the results of our measurements. Finally, Section 5 concludes this paper.

2   SIP Performance in Signaling Systems

Carrier-grade Voice-over-IP (VoIP) or multimedia networks as the one sketched in Fig. 1 include several entities that process SIP messages: For instance, calls are handled by entities realizing Call Session Control Functions (CSCF), and security screening at domain boundaries may be realized by Session Border Controllers (SBC). Even for simple actions several SIP messages have to be exchanged and processed by several entities. As a consequence, it is important to quantify the delays resulting from SIP message processing in the different entities.

2.1   SIP Proxies

In addition to the user agents in the end systems, SIP messages are processed by SIP proxies, SIP Back-to-Back User Agents (B2BUA), or network elements such as SBCs that include a proxy or B2BUA. There are different SIP proxy implementations, both commercial ones and open-source solutions. In this study, we selected the SIP Express Router (SER) [4], since it is an open source proxy that is widely deployed and known for its efficiency and high scalability.

As illustrated in Fig. 2, SER is divided into a core, which implements the basic functionalities, and so-called extensions modules. The configuration of SER is performed by a file with a shell-like syntax. This file provides so-called routes that determine the handling of received SIP messages. Additional modules extend the core functionalities, e. g. for registration. SER is completely implemented in C. The SER SIP parser is optimized for performance and uses pre-calculated 32-bit hash tables for effective parsing [5]. Because of its high-performance design SER does not parse whole SIP messages, but only the relevant parts, depending on the configuration.

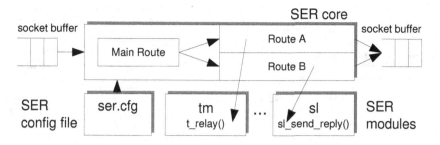

Fig. 2. Structure of the SIP Express Router

2.2 Related Work

Despite the fact that performance is important for the deployment of SIP in carrier platforms, there is only few published work that analyzes the performance of SIP proxies in depth, in particular concerning the impact of different processing steps. The performance of SIP entities largely depends on the implementation. Still, performance studies and capacity planning require at least some estimates.

A detailed study on SIP performance was published in [2]. The paper compares different proxy implementations that were specifically programmed for this study. It is reported there that the parsing needs about 25 % of the processing time, and that the total processing time of a single SIP message ranges between 1.8 and 0.2 ms. In [6] the performance of the JAIN SIP stack has been measured and call setup delays have been determined. The latency of J2EE SIP application servers is studied in [7]. However, these measurements only consider the proxy as black box, and the effort of different SIP processing functions has not been considered in detail. Other simulation studies either take the service time in proxies just as a variable (e. g., [8]), or simply make some assumptions [9].

There are also discussions on using alternative encodings for session signaling, such as type-length-value or XML. A recent example is [3]. It mainly depends on the parsing whether such formats improve the performance compared to the UTF-8 encoded text format of SIP. In the rest of this paper, the SER parsing is analyzed, which quantifies the maximum potential saving of such alternatives.

3 Measurement Setup

3.1 Testbed

For our measurements we developed a testbed that allows to measure the performance of SER by using different tools under varying parameters. Its structure is shown in Fig. 3. We use two SIPp load generators [10] to emulate the User Agents and to generate the SIP messages. We configured the two load generators so that they exchange the SIP message sequence shown in Fig. 4. They communicate over the SER SIP proxy with each other. As transport protocol for

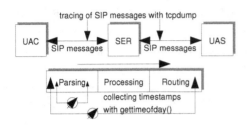

Fig. 3. Structure of the test bed

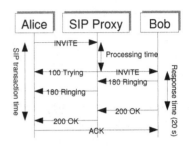

Fig. 4. Signaling flow for a SIP transaction to establish a session between two entities

SIP we use UDP. The configuration of the SER for the measurements was rudimentary, for example, without Authentication, Authorization and Accounting (AAA) functions. This allows to isolate the effects from the SIP processing of SER, as it prevents the influence of auxiliary protocols like RADIUS and DNS. The computers with SER and the load generators are connected via 100 Mbit/s FastEthernet interfaces. We use a Pentium IV 2.8 GHz with 2 GB RAM and a SUN Solaris Workstation with two Ultrasparc III+ 1 GHz processors with 2 GB RAM for comparison. It must be noted that under Solaris we use the gcc compiler for compilation of the SER, not an optimizing SUN C compiler.

3.2   Measurement Methodology

There are many different metrics to quantify SIP performance [11]. In this paper, we focus on the delay of a single SIP proxy. We study the sojourn time, i.e., the processing delay in the proxy (see Fig. 3). This is a critical metric because the summation of processing delays contributes to the total signaling delay.

We use three different methods to analyze the performance of the SER: First, we use tcpdump to capture Ethernet frames. In order to quantify the time the SIP message spent in the computer hosting SER, we calculate the difference of the time stamps from Ethernet frames carrying SIP INVITE messages from and to SER. Second, we inserted "gettimeofday()" statements in the source code of the SER to measure the time that is needed for interesting code sections, in particular around the parsing and the total processing code section. Finally we use a profiler to collect data at run-time. From the network's point of view, the data collected with tcpdump is the most important one because this is the delay SIP messages experience traveling through the proxy.

Our measurements include certain systematic errors: When the code is extended for measurements, these extensions have to be executed, which costs time. Moreover, the accuracy of the "gettimeofday()" function is limited. The accuracy of tcpdump time stamps is limited, too, and there are also small errors due to media access. The results of the run-time profiler analysis are only relative performance values because the profiler extends the machine code extensively.

4 Measurement Results

With the testbed presented in the last section we performed measurements to investigate major influence factors on SIP proxy performance. We could identify three main factors for the performance of the SER: The format of the used SIP messages, the operating system, and the configuration of SER.

4.1 Internal and External Processing Times

The external processing times are derived from time stamps of Ethernet frames. They differ from the internal processing time determined with the "gettimeof-day()" function. This is because the host's CPU is not only needed by the SER process, but also by the operating system for handling Ethernet frames and for executing other processes.

In Fig. 5, the external and internal processing times and the parse time are shown as functions of the rate of SIP INVITE messages. As to be expected, the parsing time determined by the "gettimeofday()" functions is load independent. The internal processing time is slightly load dependent. A possible reason for this is the interruption of the SER process by the Network Interface Card (NIC) when receiving Ethernet frames. However, the external processing time is highly load dependent. It grows from 200 μs to over 4 ms for 2000 Call Attempts Per Second (CAPS). The share of time needed for parsing related to the internal processing time is in the range of 20 to 33 %.

The results of the profiler analysis is illustrated in Tab. 1. Our measurement confirm the results of [2]: 25 % of the time is needed for parsing. The main share of 50 % is needed for the stateful forwarding of SIP request and 15 % are needed for the stateless forwarding of SIP replies. Note that the result of the profiler analysis is a superposition of SIP requests (INVITE messages; transaction stateful processing) and replies (100 Trying, 200 OK, ...; stateless processing). In contrast, the data collected with the other methods focuses on requests (INVITE messages) only.

The difference between internal and external processing time is the time spent in the system outside the SER process (e. g., operating system kernel and NIC drivers). For high rates of SIP INVITE message, the share of time needed for processing of messages in the operating system exceeds the time needed for parsing and processing of the messages inside the SER process by orders of magnitude. It can be assumed that the process scheduler of the operating system is accountable for the increase of the external processing time for higher loads, because it interrupts the processing of SIP messages through SER. However, varying the Linux kernel scheduler frequency (100 Hz, 250 Hz and 1000 Hz) did not show any significant impact.

4.2 Influence of the Format of SIP Messages

In order to study the impact of differently formatted SIP messages, we performed measurements with different SIP messages. We focus on RFC 3261 compliant messages and do not examine the influence of corrupted messages.

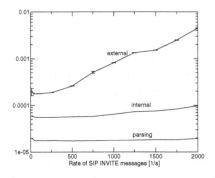

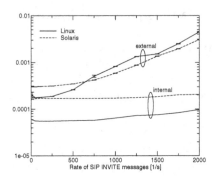

Fig. 5. External, internal processing time and parsing time (in s) for Linux

Fig. 6. Comparison of the processing times (in s) between Linux and Solaris

In Tab. 2, the parsing times for differently formatted messages are presented: Message 1 is a standard formatted SIP message. Message 2 has its via header at the end of the message. In message 3, additional header fields are inserted between the via header and the rest of the SIP message. Additional to message 3, in message 4 multi-line header fields and combination of upper case and lower case characters in the header names are used. Combination of upper and lower cases in the header names increase the number of comparisons to determine the type of the header, as multi-line header fields do.

The SER has to parse all the via headers to add its own via header at the end. One can see that the format of SIP messages has a significant influence of the parsing time. Sloppily formatted SIP messages can increase the parsing time. However, the parsing time is still clearly one or two orders of magnitude smaller than the external processing time.

4.3   Impact of the Operating System

Furthermore, we analyze the influence of the operating system in more detail. We compare Linux (kernel version 2.6.18) with Solaris (version 5.10) both with default configuration except for optimized UDP settings.

In Fig. 6, the external and internal processing times are shown as functions of the rate of SIP INVITE messages, for Linux and Solaris. The absolute values are

Table 1. Relative time shares of the processing stages collected with the profiler

Table 2. Parsing time for different formatted, RFC 3261 compliant SIP messages

Action	Share [%]
Parsing	25
Stateful processing	50
Stateless processing	15
Others	10

Load	Parse time [μs]
Message type 1	18.0
Message type 2	12.5
Message type 3	20.0
Message type 4	22.5

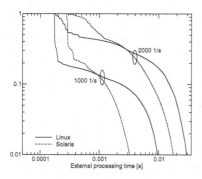

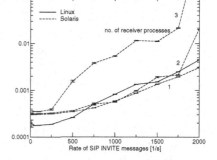

Fig. 7. CCDF of the external processing time for Linux and Solaris for 1000 and 2000 CAPS

Fig. 8. External processing time (in s) for Linux and Solaris with different number of receiver processes

not easy to compare because the hard- and software architectures of Linux/x86 and Solaris/Ultrasparc are quite different. Still, for both operating systems, the same effects can be observed: The external processing time increases with increasing of the SIP message load. It is interesting to note that for higher loads Solaris performs better in the external processing time, although the internal processing time of the Solaris system is higher than when using Linux.

So far, we have only discussed mean values of the processing time. In Fig. 7 we present the Complementary Cumulative Distribution Function (CCDF) of the external processing time for Linux and Solaris, obtained from the tcpdump time stamps. The Linux and Solaris curves are similar. For increasing load the jitter increases but the minimum external processing time keeps constant. For Linux the 95 % quantile increases from 5 ms to over 20 ms and for Solaris it increases from 2 ms to 11 ms, when the CAPS are increased from 1000 to 2000. In both systems there is a non-negligible probability of rather high delays.

4.4 Impact of the SER Configuration

In Fig. 8 the external processing time is shown as a function of the rate of SIP INVITE messages. As parameter we change the number of receiver processes. They can be adjusted by the SER configuration file. When running on Linux, the number of receiver processes has no influence on the processing time. This is why in Fig. 8 only the result for one receiver process is illustrated. However, if Solaris is used, the number of receiver processes has an impact on the processing time: It can be observed that there is a significant increase of the external processing time when the number of receiver processes exceeds the number of CPUs.

5 Conclusion and Future Work

In this paper we present detailed performance measurements for the SIP Express Router (SER). We determine three major factors influencing the performance of

SER: The format of SIP messages, the operating system, and the configuration of SER. Our results confirm previous studies, which have reported that the parsing may take up to 25 % of the internal processing effort. However, we also show that the parsing effort has a much smaller share of the external delay, which is the critical performance metric from the network's point of view. Even though this paper only considers the SER proxy, we expect that other SIP entity implementations have similar performance characteristics.

The measurements indicate that the potential for speeding up session setup by using alternative message encoding formats is rather low, in particular when there are also further delays caused by, for instance, address resolution or AAA functions. Still, since the format of SIP messages does affect the processing complexity, it could be useful to normalize SIP messages at domain boundaries, such as to re-arrange headers in order to reduce processing efforts in core SIP proxies.

Our measurements results have been obtained from a simple network setup. A further step would be to perform measurements in a complete signaling scenario with AAA functions and other auxiliary protocols, e. g., in a full IMS setup.

References

1. Camarillo, G., García-Martín, M.A.: The 3G IP Multimedia Subsystem (IMS): Merging the Internet and the Cellular Worlds, 2nd edn. Wiley, Chichester (2005)
2. Cortez, M., Ensor, J.R., Esteban, J.O.: On SIP Performance. Bell Labs Technical Journal 9(3), 155–172 (2004)
3. Baset, S., Schulzrinne, H.: Peer-to-Peer Protocol (P2PP). IETF Internet Draft, work in progress (February 2007)
4. SIP Express Router (SER): http://www.iptel.org/ser/
5. Janak, J., Kuthan, J.: SIP Express Router v0.8.8 - Developer's Guide. FhG Fokus (2002)
6. Gokhale, S.S., Lu, J.: Signaling Performance of SIP Based VoIP: A Measurment-Based Approach. In: Proc. IEEE Globecom, IEEE Computer Society Press, Los Alamitos (November 2005)
7. Van Den Bossche, B., De Turck, F., Dhoedt, B., Demeester, P., Maas, G., Moreels, J., Van Vlerken, B., Pollet, T.: J2EE-based Middleware for Low Latency Service Enabling Platforms. In: Proc. IEEE Globecom, IEEE Computer Society Press, Los Alamitos (November 2006)
8. Gurbani, V.K., Jagadeesan, L.J., Menditratta, V.B.: Characterizing Session Initiation Protocol (SIP) Network Performance and Reliability. In: Malek, M., Nett, E., Suri, N. (eds.) ISAS 2005. LNCS, vol. 3694, pp. 196–211. Springer, Heidelberg (2005)
9. Kist, A.A., Harris, R.J.: SIP Signalling Delay in 3GPP. In: Proc. IFIP International Symposium on Communication Interworking (2002)
10. Gayraud, R., Jaques, O., et al.: SIPp - SIP Load Generator, http://sipp.sourceforge.net/index.html
11. Malas, D.: SIP End-to-End Performance Metrics. IETF Internet Draft, work in progress (January 2007)

A Novel Loop-Free IP Fast Reroute Algorithm

Gábor Enyedi, Gábor Rétvári, and Tibor Cinkler

High Speed Networks Laboratory,
Department of Telecomunications and Media Informatics,
Budapest University of Technology and Economics
H-1117, Magyar Tudósok körútja 2., Budapest, Hungary
{enyedi, retvari, cinkler}@tmit.bme.hu

Abstract. Although providing reliable network services is getting more and more important, currently used methods in IP networks are typically reactive and error correcting can take a long time. One of the most interesting solutions is interface based fast rerouting, where not only the destination address but also the incoming interface is taken into account during the forwarding. Unfortunately, current methods can not handle all the possible situations as they are prone to form loops and make parts of the network with no failure unavailable. In this paper we propose a new interface based routing method, which always avoids loops for the price of a bit longer paths. We also present extensive simulation results to compare current and proposed algorithms.

Keywords: IPFRR, IP, fast, reroute, routing, interface.

1 Introduction

In the last few decades Internet has become one of the world's most significant communication systems. Although fault tolerance was always one of the most important attributes of this network, using the traditional resilience mechanism of IP usually needs significant time to converge. However, convergance times should decrease. With the growing of networks the time of transients between the failure and reconfiguration is getting longer, and today this convergence can even take some minutes.

The main reason of this slow reconfiguration is the reactive approach for recovery of a failure taken by conventional routing protocols, like the Open Shortest Path First (OSPF) or the Intermediate System-to-Intermediate System (IS-IS) routing protocol used ubiquitously in modern IP networks. Here, fault recovery is assured by recomputing the routing tables at each router after a failure shows up, which might take significant time.

In contrast to traditional IP error correction techniques, which are fundamentally reactive, the new IP Fast Reroute (IPFRR) framework proposes proactive solutions, so these methods are always ready to reroute packets. Naturally this reroute must be done *locally* because there is no time for any communication. Using these algorithms transient link errors can also be avoided; since packets can reach the destination, the starting of reconfiguration of the network can be delayed, so it can be done if the persistence of the failure is sure.

A. Pras and M. van Sinderen (Eds.): EUNICE 2007, LNCS 4606, pp. 111–119, 2007.

The simplest proactive solutions only work in some special networks. For example, Equal Cost Multiple Path (ECMP) [1] can use multiple shortest paths to a destination, if exists, and is able to shift traffic from a failed shortest path to another one, unaffected by the failure. Routers using Loop-Free Alternates (LFAs) [2], another IPFRR technique, need a neighbor with a shotest path not containing the failed resource. Improved version of this method [3] needs a reachable node from where the destination can be reached, and packets are tunneled to this new node. The first solution that promises 100% fault recovery is Not-Via addresses [4]. Here, each interface has two addresses, and the second one means that the link is down, so packets are tunneled on a path to the next hop, which bypasses the failed link.

One of the most interesting possibilities is interface based routing. These methods use both the address of the destination and the incoming interface for selecting the next hop. Using this extra information Failure Insensitive Routing (FIR) [5] does not need significantly new hardware and it can survive single link failures. Although the authors presented two algorithms, the computed routings are the same, so we refer to these as FIR in the next part of this paper.

Unfortunately, FIR can create loops when more than one link or at least one node is unavailable (a loop is a forwarding cycle, which is never left by packets, and packets are dropped when TTL is up). Loops have usually serious effects. When a loop exists in a network even those parts of the system can become unavailable, where all the resources are operable, because the high load increases the probability of losing packets. In this paper we give a possible solution of this problem, based on the observation that loops can be avoided if not always the shortest paths are used in normal operation.

The rest of this paper is organized as follows: in Section 2 we prove that FIR can create loops. In Section 3 we present a novel routing solution, which can tolerate single link failures and never creates loops. In Section 4 we discuss implementation questions and in Section 5 we compare the current and the proposed algorithms using simulation results. In the last section we summarize our results.

2   Loops Using FIR

It was mentioned previously and proved in [5] that it is possible to correct one link failure with FIR in a network using interface-based routing. First, we recall the algorithm of FIR then we show that FIR can create loops.

The base idea of FIR is simple: if a node gets a packet from a neighbor which usually does not use this direction for forwarding, then there is a failure in the network. FIR calculates which links could have been failed and also – if it is possible to avoid them – another path to the destination. Using this information, FIR precomputes an alternative route for each incoming interface which is guaranteed to avoid the failed links. It is important to mention that if all the links are available FIR uses shortest paths for forwarding.

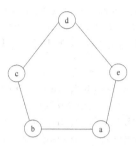
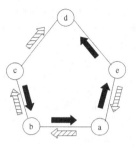

Fig. 1. A network with ring topology   **Fig. 2.** The two arborescences of LFIR

Although this method is very effective it has some serious drawbacks because of the behavior when no failure exists. Theorem 1 shows this. For purposes of this paper, we call a routing *optimal* if packets are always forwarded along shortest paths if all the links are available. A routing is *failure insensitive* if traffic can pass between all nodepairs even if one link is down. We call a routing *loop-free*, if there is no loop even if any subset of links and/or nodes has failed.

Theorem 1. *There are some networks where no optimal, failure insensitive and loop-free interface-based routing exists.*

Proof. See network on Fig. 1, which uses an optimal and failure insensitive interface-based routing, and let all the lengths of the links be 1. Let link $\{e, d\}$ and $\{c, d\}$ be both unavailable. It is easy to see that packets heading from a to d will be sent to e because the routing is optimal. Naturally e will send packets on path $e - a - b - c$ because failure insensitive interface-based routing is used. Because $\{c, d\}$ is down and c is the default next hop of b – so c "thinks" $\{c, d\}$ is the first unavailable link –, c tries to correct the error and packets are sent back following path $c - b - a - e$. So a routing loop is formed between nodes e and c, which completes the proof of the theorem.   □

Because FIR is interface based, optimal and failure-insensitive Theorem 1 proves, that there are some networks where using FIR can cause loops. Section 5 shows that these networks are not rare; FIR can cause loop in most networks.

3   Loop-Free Fast Interface-Based Routing

It was shown in the previous section that FIR can create loops. In this section, we propose a novel technique, Loop-Free Failure Insensitive Routing (LFIR), which can solve this problem. Naturally LFIR is not an optimal routing. First we deal with the problem of 2-edge-connected networks (networks with two edge-disjoint paths between each nodes), then we discuss an improved version of the first algorithm, where 2-edge-connectivity is not necessary.

In the rest of this paper we refer to the set of vertices of graph G as $V(G)$ and the set of edges as $E(G)$. If there is an edge between a and b we refer to this as $\{a, b\}$, if it is an undirected edge, or (a, b) if it is a directed one (a is the source, b is the target).

The basic idea of LFIR is to find paths from each node to each destination in such a way that when a node gets a packet from a specific incoming interface, it can always decide if either the default path was used or the packet is on a detour due to a failed link. If the detour has also failed, the packet must be dropped. To do this we must recall a special version of a theorem of Edmonds which comes easily from [6].

Definition 1. *A branching (spanning arborescence) rooted at vertex d in digraph G is a spanning tree directed in such a way, that each vertex $x \neq d$ has one edge going out. (Note that branchings are usually defined in the reverse direction.)*

Proposition 1. *Let G be a digraph, which is 2-edge-connected. It is possible to find two edge-disjoint branchings in this graph rooted at any $d \in V(G)$.*

One may observe that a branching is something like routing for a given destination d; if a packet can follow the directed edges of a branching rooted at d it reaches the destination. The only difficulty is that links can be used in both directions, so it can be modeled with an undirected graph.

It is possible to solve this problem. Let G be the undirected 2-edge-connected graph of a network. Let G' be a directed graph such that $V(G) = V(G')$ and if $\{i, j\} \in E(G)$ then $(i, j) \in E(G')$ and $(j, i) \in E(G')$. It can be easily proven that G' is also 2-edge-connected.

Now, the version of LFIR for 2-edge-connected networks is the following. Convert the undirected graph G to a digraph G', find two edge-disjoint branchings in G' rooted at d for all $d \in V(G')$. For each destination label the two branchings (1 and 2). When a packet arrives following a particular branching (the destination contained by the packet and the incoming interface shows which branching is that), forward it following the same one if it is possible – there is exactly one outgoing edge of a branching at each node. If it is not possible and the packet used the first branching, try to forward it following the second one; if it used the second one, drop the packet. Use the first branching at the first hop, if it is possible. The routing for d (which consists of the two branchings) is shown in Fig. 2. The next theorem shows that packets always reach the destination if at most one link is down and that loops can never be created.

Theorem 2. *The version of LFIR used in 2-edge-connected networks is correct (it never creates forwarding loop) and complete (packets arrive if at most one link is down).*

Proof. It is easy to see that packets can travel on each link at most two times – once using branching one and once using branching two –, so there can not be a forwarding loop. It is also easy to see that packets arrive to the destination along branching one if all the links are available.

Now suppose that exactly one link, $\{i, j\} \in E(G)$ is failed. Naturally $(i, j) \in E(G')$ and $(j, i) \in E(G')$ and these two edges can not belong to the same branching, because there is no cycle in branchings. Suppose that a packet can not reach the destination. First it is forwarded along the first branching. However its forwarding failed, so it was tried to use link $\{i, j\}$ which means that either (i, j) or (j, i) is in the first branching. Without loss of generality, we can suppose that this edge is (i, j). So the packet has left node i using the second branching. Failing the forwarding again means that link $\{i, j\}$ was tried to be used again, so (j, i) is an edge of the second branching. But the packet could reach node j from node i meaning that there is a path from i to j in the second branching and with (j, i) there is a cycle which contradicts the assumption that there is no cycle in a branching.   □

Next we deal with the problem of non-2-edge-connected networks. If the network is not 2-edge-connected two edge-disjoint branchings can not be found, but correcting the errors of those links, which do not cause the network to fall into two parts is still possible.

An undirected graph can be partitioned into z disjunct components, such that these components are 2-edge-connected. Naturally, it is possible that some componets contain only one vertex. If leaving a link causes the network to fall into two parts, it means that this link – a bridge – is between two 2-edge-connected components. It is also true that if vertices s and d are not in the same 2-edge-connected component, there is only one edge-disjoint path between them.

Using these ideas one may observe a possibility to improve LFIR. Duplicate the bridges virtually in the graph of the network. This new graph is 2-edge-connected, so after the transformation to a directed graph there will be at least two edge-disjoint branchings. Packets can follow these branchings as before. If a packet following a branching crosses a bridge, then the node after the bridge can not decide which branching was used, so use the first one for the next forwarding.

It can be easily proven that all the bridges are used by both branchings and each is used in the same direction in the directed graph (i.e. if $\{i, j\}$ is a bridge, then both branchings contain (i, j) or both contain (j, i)).

Theorem 3. *The improved version of LFIR is correct and complete (packet will arrive if at most one non-bridge link is down).*

Proof. If there is no failure packets follow the first branching and d (the root) is reached. If one link used by branching one is down, and it is not a bridge, packets either reach node d – if it is in the same component (because of Theorem 2) – or leave the 2-edge-connected component following the second branching, and after that they will reach d following the first branching. The algorithm is complete.

Now suppose that the algorithm is not correct. If there is a forwarding loop, there must be more than one failed link or at least one failed node, because the algorithm is complete. First suppose that all the nodes are available. In this case it is true that the forwarding loop must leave at least one 2-edge-connected component because of Theorem 2. So there must be a component – let it be component A – that packets leave and then return to it. Let 2-edge-connected component B be the last component which was left before packet returns to A. There must be a bridge $\{i, j\}$ such that $i \in A$ and $j \in B$. Because each bridge is used in the same direction there is one (j, i) and no (i, j) edge in both branchings, so the packet did not leave A using bridge $\{i, j\}$. But his means there is a path from component A to component B without edge $\{i, j\}$, and another with $\{i, j\}$ which contradicts the assumption that $\{i, j\}$ is a bridge.

Node failure can be treated like some link failures. If the source is available and some nodes go down it has the same effect as all the links of these nodes become unavailable, so the algorithm is correct. Naturally, if the source is down it can not send any packet.   □

4   Implementation Questions

In the previous section we proposed an algorithm for constructing a loop-free failure insensitive routing. In this section, we discuss some implementation questions which are still open.

Finding branchings: For LFIR the most important is an effective algorithm for finding branchings. Note that, unlike the ones in the literature, our branchings are directed *towards* the destination, not *away* from it. However, this does not cause any problem since any algorithm described below can be twaeked to reverse the direction of the branchings found. The fastest algorithm – known by the authors – was proposed by Tarjan [7], and it needs $O(e\alpha(e, n))$ time, where $e = |E(G)|$, $n = |V(G)|$ and $\alpha(e, n)$ is a very slowly growing function related to the inverse of Ackerman's function. The value of this function is practically a constant. Although these methods are very fast, we have used an algorithm of Lovász [8]. This algorithm is simple and fast enough for our purposes (it takes only $O(e^2)$ steps to find two branchings with breadth first search). But more importantly, Lovász's algorithm allows us to apply a quick heuristic to decrease the length of the paths in the primary branching (used as the default path, i.e., when there are no errors): we always choose the directed edge from the set of edges that can be added to the arborescence, which provides the shortest path to the target of this edge. Using binary heap with this heuristic $O(e^2 \log e)$ time is needed.

Finding bridges: If it is not sure that the network is at least 2-edge-connected, it is needed to find the bridges. Finding bridges can be done in $O(e\alpha(e, n))$ [7] time, but this algorithm is complicated. We used to check if all the nodes are reachable after leaving an edge with a breadth first search. If not, the selected link is a bridge. This needs $O(e^2)$ time.

Using LFIR in distributed environment: Using LFIR in distributed environment – such as routers in a network – raise a new problem; routers must find the same two branchings. A unique priority given to all the edges can solve this problem. If there are more edges with the same distance from the root during the edge selection, choose always the one with the highest priority. In this way building a branching is fully defined, so if the routers have the same information about the network the same routing will be calculated.

5   Simulation Results

In the previous sections algorithm LFIR was presented. Although it was discussed that using this algorithm loops can be avoided for the price of using longer paths in normal operation, the probability of loops using FIR and the lengths of path using LFIR are still unknown. In this section, we answer these two questions.

During all the simulations we used the topology of real networks – the NSF network [9] and the backbone network of Germany and Italy [10]. To make these networks random we used random edge lengths; the distribution of lengths was independent, discrete and uniform between 1 and 50. We presumed that FIR drops packets only if it can't forward them (edge of detour is down).

Table 1. Average probability of loops when two edges or one node is down

Top.	Prob. of loops w/ failed edges	Prob. of loops w/ failed node
NSF	5.37 %	74.45 %
Germany	10.04 %	90.62 %
Italy	4.2 %	83.5 %

Table 2. Average path lengths using LFIR related to using shortest paths

Top.	LFIR w/ heur.	LFIR w/o heur.
NSF	106.27 %	137.37 %
Germany	116.36 %	146.15 %
Italy	112.07 %	150.38 %

In the first and second simulations we studied the possibility of loops in networks. We used random experiments to decide if it is possible to remove exactly two links – first simulation – or exactly one node – second simulation – from the random network such a way that FIR makes loop. These experiments can be modeled by a Bernoulli random variable, so it can be proven using Chebyshev's inequality that after 250000 experiments a symmetrical confidence interval with size 0.02 (the difference between the real probability and the approximated is at most 1%) at level 99% can be calculated.

The result of these simulations is surprising: it was always possible to create loop with FIR in all the studied topologies irrespectively of the given lengths of edges – all the probabilities were 100%. Naturally this means only that network topologies in which FIR is prone to forming routing loops are quite common, not that FIR can create loop in all networks.

In the third and fourth simulations, we studied the probability that loops show up when using FIR. Therefore, we conducted another experiment to decide if there is a loop in a given random network if two randomly selected links or one randomly selected node is down. The confidence interval is the same as previous.

The result of these simulations is presented in Table 1. Curiously, the probability of FIR forming loops is not negligible, above all if it is a node that fails $(75 - 90\%)$ and not a link $(4 - 10\%)$. We believe that this experiment evidences that, without clever modifications, FIR is prone to forming routing loops in case of a multiple link or single node failure. Fortunately, LFIR is guaranteed to avoid loops at the cost of an insignificant growth in the average path lengths, as testified by the simulations in the following.

To answer the question of path lengths calculated by LFIR we made 250000 random experiments with each topology. We calculated the average path lengths to each destination using LFIR – with and without heuristic (Section 4) – and shortest paths, and the quotient of these path lengths were summed. In this way we calculated the average ratio between the two methods. Results are found on Table 2. It can be observed that the greatest increase of average length of paths is only 16 %, which is low enough to let most networks use LFIR.

6   Conclusions

In this paper, we discussed methods for interface-based fast IP rerouting, a new type of proactive routing technique insensitive to link failures. We have shown that the FIR algorithm has the disadvantage that it can create routing loops – which has usually devastating effects – when more failed links or failed nodes are present. Our simulation results show that, depending on the specifics of a network, forming such loops can become quite common. We gave a formal proof that routing loops in FIR can be attributed to the fact that it uses shortest paths when there is no failure in the network. Based on this observation, we proposed LFIR, a novel failure insensitive routing solution. LFIR basically achieves a trade-off between optimality and correctness: it guarantees loopfree error recovery while, at the same time, it increases the length of the default paths. We presented extensive simulation studies to show that this increase of path lengths is tolerable (less than 16% in average). Our results indicate LFIR can bring important benefits to almost all IP networks, where a small surplus of capacity is present to accommodate the slightly longer routes.

References

1. Thaler, D.: Multipath issues in unicast and multicast next-hop selection. Internet Engineering Task Force: RFC 2991 (November 2000)
2. Atlas, A.: Loop-free alternates for ip/ldp local protection. Internet Draft (March 2005), available online: http://tools.ietf.org/html/draft-ietf-rtgwg-ipfrr-spec-base-00
3. Bryant, S., Filsfils, C., Previdi, S., Shand, M.: Ip fast-reroute using tunnels. Internet Draft (April 2005), available online: http://tools.ietf.org/html, http://draft-bryant-ipfrr-tunnels-02
4. Bryant, S., Shand, M., Previdi, S.: Ip fast reroute using not-via addresses. Internet Draft (December 2006), available online:http://www.ietf.org/internet-drafts/draft-ietf-rtgwg-ipfrr-notvia-addre sses-00.txt
5. Nelakuditi, S., Lee, S., Yu, Y., Zhang, Z.-L., Chuah, C-N.: Fast local rerouting for handling transient link failures. Accepted for publication in IEEE/ACM Transactions on Networking (December 2006), available online: http://arena.cse.sc.edu/papers/fir.ton.pdf

6. Edmonds, J.: Edge-disjoint branchings. Combinatorial Algorithms, 91–96 (1973)
7. Tarjan, R.E.: Edge-disjoint spanning trees and depth-first search. Inf. Proc. Letters 3(2), 51–53 (1974)
8. Lovász, L.: On two minimax theorems in graph theory. Journal of Combinatorial Theory, 96–103 (1976)
9. Chinoy, B., Braun, H.W.: The national science foundation network. Tech. Rep., CAIDA (September 1992), available online: http://www.caida.org/outreach/papers/1992/nsfn/nsfnet-t1-technology.pdf
10. Garcia-Osma, M.L.: TID scenarios for advanced resilience. Tech. Rep., The NOBEL Project, Work Package 2, Activity A.2.1 (September 2005)

A Simulation-Based Study of TCP Performance over an Optical Burst Switched Backbone with 802.11 Access

Isaias Martinez-Yelmo, Ignacio Soto, David Larrabeiti, and Carmen Guerrero

Universidad Carlos III de Madrid, 28911, Leganes (Madrid), Spain
{imyelmo, isoto, dlarra, guerrero}@it.uc3m.es

Abstract. The combined effect of optical and wireless subnetworks in an hypothetical future scenario where core networks have evolved to the still prototype Optical Burst Switching (OBS) technology is an open research issue.

This paper studies this hybrid scenario, in the particular case of 802.11 access, by reviewing the key aspects of OBS and 802.11 with an impact on the performance of TCP, and makes a simulation-based assessment of the relative influence of both technologies over the effective end-to-end behaviour of TCP.

1 Introduction

The exploitation of Dense Wavelength Division Multiplexing (DWDM) as a dynamic Optical Circuit Switching technology (OCS), where lightpaths are optically switched to interconnect the backbone edge nodes, has just started. This technology removes the opto-electronic conversion bottleneck in the core of the network and provides the full capacity of an optical carrier to transport data edge to edge. However, it yields no statistical time multiplexing gain of lightpath capacity and connectivity is constrained by the number of optical carriers provided by DWDM. This limitation will eventually be overcome when Optical Packet Switching (OPS) is technologically feasible. In the meantime, Optical Burst Switching [1] seems to be the key transition technology on the way to Optical Packet Switching (OPS).

On the other hand, wireless LAN (WLAN) access is becoming increasingly popular for personal broadband communications, and is envisaged as a real alternative to the widespread Third Generation (3G) Mobile System. One of the most widely deployed WLAN technologies is the IEEE Standard 802.11b. A lot of work has been devoted to the analysis of TCP/IP performance over 802.11 e.g. [2], [3]. However, up to the date, no study on the relative impact of OBS and 802.11 together on TCP has been realised in a scenario like the one shown in Fig.1. This scenario, interworking with electronically packet-switched subnetworks - assumed over-provisioned in our study to focus on the relative effects of WLAN and OBS -, might become a reality in the next future. A comparative study is hence relevant because the behaviour of both technologies is quite different with respect to delay and packet loss.

The structure of the paper is the following. Section 2 is a short review of factors driving the performance of TCP. Sections 3 and 4 are devoted to outline the effects of 802.11b and OBS over TCP respectively. Then, section 5 presents a simulation-based analysis of TCP performance on a Wireless LAN access network connected to an OBS core network. Finally, section 6 draws the conclusions.

A. Pras and M. van Sinderen (Eds.): EUNICE 2007, LNCS 4606, pp. 120–127, 2007.

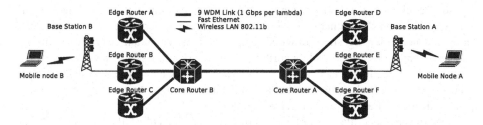

Fig. 1. OBS - WLAN simulation scenario

2   TCP Congestion Control

Basically, TCP has a byte-oriented sliding window mechanism to dynamically adapt the data rate to the network state. An End-to-End mechanism exists to avoid congestion in the network where only the transmitter and the receiver take part. The Congestion Control mechanism of TCP is ruled by several parameters [2]:

- **The lower window edge** ($Wmin(t)$)**:** All data numbered up to and including $Wmin(t) - 1$ has been transmitted and ACKed. $Wmin(t)$ is non-decreasing variable; the receipt of an ACK with sequence number $n > Wmin(t)$ causes $Wmin(t)$ to jump to n.
- **Congestion Window** ($W(t)$)**:** The sender can send packets with a sequence number n where $Wmin(t) \leq n < Wmin(t) + W(t)$ where $W(t) \leq Wmax$ where Wmax is the maximum transmission window.
- **Slow Start threshold** ($Wth(t)$)**:** This value serves to set an inflexion point in the growth of the congestion window from geometric to lineal (congestion avoidance region).

The behaviour of TCP congestion control defines two working regions:

- **Slow Start:** If $W < Wth(t)$, each first ACK implies that $W(t+1) = W(t) + 1$
- **Congestion Avoidance:** If $W \geq Wth(t)$, each first ACK implies that $W(t+1) = W(t) + 1/W(t)$.

TCP estimates with each first ACK received the maximum RTT of the ongoing connection (called Retransmission TimeOut - RTO) and with this value a timer is started. Depending on the version of TCP running on the transmitter, the congestion window W and the Slow Start threshold Wth are modified in a different way if the RTO time expires or duplicated ACKs are received. For a detailed explanation see [4], [5] and [6]. Depending on the version of TCP, different performance will be obtained in a particular scenario.

3   TCP on Wireless LAN 802.11

Most commercial Wireless LAN products are based on the IEEE 802.11 standards.

For the purpose of this paper, it is necessary to understand the basic behaviour of TCP over an 802.11b network. In-depth performance studies can be found in [7], [8]. The performance of TCP is severely hindered by packet losses due to interferences, noise or collisions. This well-known fact is due to the assumptions made in the design of TCP, where an RTO timer expiration or the reception of duplicated ACKs are interpreted as network congestion. In wired scenarios the transmission error probability is very low, and packet loss is solely attributed to network congestion. However, in wireless technologies, losses are usually due to interferences and noise, and delay is not necessarily due to link congestion but to retransmissions following a frame error; thus, TCP reduces the transmission rate erroneously.

A good analysis of the performance of different versions of TCP over lossy links is provided in [3] and [2]. This latter work shows that the most recent implementations of TCP perform better on lossy links because the **congestion window** is not decreased drastically under packet loss. Other works focus on performance improvement [9], [10].

4   Optical Burst Switching

4.1   Overview

Next generation core networks are planned to be based on DWDM technology using Optical Circuit Switching featuring real lightwave switching. The problem comes in large core networks, where the number of available lightpaths becomes insufficient to build fully-meshed OCS networks. Statistical time multiplexing is hence required to achieve scalability and efficiency, either by means of optical traffic grooming or by Optical Burst Switching (OBS) [1].

The idea of OBS is achieving statistical time multiplexing at the optical layer but taking into account the current physical limits of the optical switching technology. Current optical switching laboratory prototypes take a few milliseconds to change the state of a light beam switch. This speed is insufficient to switch packets optically at Terabits per second. OBS is a practical trade-off between OCS and OPS whereby statistical multiplexing is obtained with a coarser granularity. The proposal in OBS is to use larger-than-packets switching units to keep up efficiency; this way most of the time is spent on transmitting data and less on changing the switch state. These large switching units are called *"bursts"*: a group of packets that leave the OBS network at the same egress router; all the packets are encapsulated in the ingress router and the OBS burst is configured with a label to the destination address of the desired egress router. Finally, the egress router takes the received OBS burst, decapsulates the packets and forwards the packets electronically according to the routing table.

Since switching time is long in current optical switches, the transmission of a burst is preceded by a control packet named *Burst Header Packet* (BHP) whose purpose is reserving resources for the transmission of the burst through the OBS switches. This control packet is sent over a signalling channel to be electronically processed at each hop. If due to existing traffic, the burst cannot be scheduled to be transmitted in a free slot in one of the output wavelengths, the OBS burst is dropped. At each node a heuristic scheduling algorithm is used to allocate the necessary resources for the bursts to reach the next hop, [11].

Delay and jitter can be controlled as follows. Packets are buffered according to their egress router and they are transmitted all together in a burst. The transmission of a burst could be realised according two configuration configuration parameters:

- *Burst Threshold:* Maximum number of packest that can be transmitted in a burst. Thus, if this value is reached, the corresponding burst should be transmitted immediately. If this value is reached earlier, the waiting queue time will be smaller, and the delay will be also smaller.
- *Burst Timeout:* A bust will be transmitted if this timeout expires although the burst threshold has not be reached. Thus, this timeout guarantees a maximum value of delay introduced by the OBS network. A longer burst timeout implies less average delay but less network utilisation efficiency.

4.2 Key Issues on TCP over OBS

There are several works that analyse the performance of TCP in OBS networks, for instance [12]. This performance is closely related with the Retransmission timeout (RTO) of TCP and how the different versions of TCP treat this event [13]. Nevertheless, several qualitative general considerations can be made to understand the way OBS affects TCP.

The rate of a TCP connection can be approximated to the value of the TCP transmission Window Size divided by the Round Trip Time (RTT). The RTT of a connection crossing an OBS network is related to the value assigned to the Burst Size and Burst Timeout parameters. The RTT decreases with the value of these parameters, since it takes less time to send the OBS burst. The Burst size is the dominant parameter for a heavy loaded destination egress node because OBS bursts are sent as soon as the Burst size is reached. On the other hand, the Burst Timeout is the dominant parameter in a link with low load of traffic due to the fact that data is delivered only when the Burst Timeout timer expires.

Furthermore, it must be taken into consideration how the OBS network can affect the TCP Window Size. The size of the TCP Window is set according to different events depending on the TCP version used, upon two events: RTO and Duplicated ACKs, both events produced by packet losses. Losses of packets in an OBS network are due to OBS burst drops when these cannot be allocated in a free transmission time. This blocking probability depends on the available wavelengths for data and signalling, on the patterns of the incoming traffic and on the Burst Timeout and Burst Size parameters; but it is not easy to measure how all these parameters can affect the Window Size and throughput without simulation [12].

5   TCP Performance in an 802.11b Access Network Connected to an OBS Core Network

To the date, no previous study related with the relative impact of OBS and WLAN on TCP performance has been realised. Both technologies drop packets for different reasons: both for high load in the network and, in the case of WLAN, also for bad link conditions. A simulation study of the effects of both technologies is a first step to understand the interaction, eventual combined effects and overall performance achieved.

5.1   NS-2 Configuration

The simulation tool used to simulate the designed scenario is the NS-2 simulator [14] with an extension to simulate OBS networks used in [12] featuring the burst scheduler presented in [11]. The propagation model used in the wireless link is the *shadowing model* [15]. This model allows to approximate the Error Probability of a Wireless LAN link in different indoor and outdoor scenarios. Since the purpose of the simulation is comparing the relative effects of the WLAN and OBS losses together on TCP, the wired access network between the WLAN network and OBS core is assumed to be over-provisioned. Thus, the scenario under study is shown in Fig.1. Mobile nodes have 802.11b interfaces at 11 Mbps whereas the OBS network has nine wavelengths between each node working at 1 Gbps, two of them dedicated for signalling. WLAN losses happen on the link between base station A and mobile node A.

The methodology used is very similar to the one applied in [12]. Since the simulation of many background individual simultaneous connections has a high cost, its effect in the core has been modelled by means of self-similar background traffic, considering that Internet traffic has been widely characterised with this distribution probability [16]. The parameters used for the self-similar traffic have been 10000 batchs per second, a Hurst exponent for arrival of 0.5 and a Hurst exponent size of 0.5. The values of the Hurst parameters has been set to be conservative. Different batch sizes have been used to increase the background traffic and OBS blocking probability (OBS Pb). These patterns have been configured between each edge router in the proposed scenario.

The *Burst timeout* has been set to 0.01 seconds and the *Burst size* has been configured to 70,000 bytes. Furthermore, 5 Fiber Delay Lines (FDLs) of 0.1 ms have been placed in each core node to get better link utilisation for a given burst drop probability. Finally, the TCP NewReno variant has been used for the simulation as this is the most widely used in Internet [17]. Furthermore, this variant has proved to give the best performance on lossy links [2].

5.2   TCP Performance Under 802.11b and OBS Networks

This section presents the results obtained in the simulation. Fig.2 displays a three dimensional plot of the overall throughput with respect to the packet drop probabilities in the Wireless LAN and OBS networks. The dropping probabilities in the OBS network have been obtained by configuring different batch sizes of the self-similar sources to obtain different background traffics between each edge router. It can be seen how the throughput decreases exponentially as the WLAN dropping probability grows. More interestingly, the graph shows that OBS has a minor influence on the overall throughput in a range of dropping probability values (e.g. [0..0.01]) where WLAN by itself brings the performance down to a 50%.

Several cuts on the three dimensional figure have been made and are represented in Fig.3 on logarithmic scale. The plots include the confidence intervals for a confidence of 95%. The comparison of plots A and B gives evidence of the different response to losses in each subnetwork. Plot B shows the way the WLAN determines the maximum overall throughput that can be reached for a wider range of OBS drop probabilities, always modulated by the state of the OBS network.

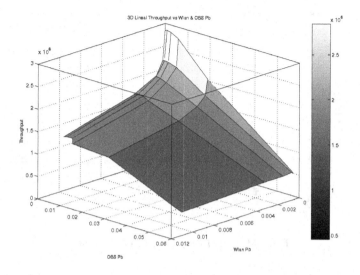

Fig. 2. 3D Mean Throughput Graphic

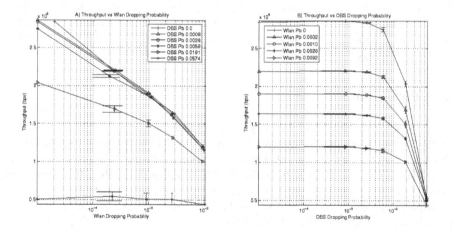

Fig. 3. Mean Throughput Graphic

At first sight, the expected behaviour would be a monotonously decreasing curve with the OBS packet dropping probability. However, when the OBS dropping probability increases, the throughput does not decrease in a significant way before the OBS packet dropping probability is over a given value. Fig.3 shows that this performance-fall value is $5 \cdot 10^{-3}$ in our sample case. This makes WLAN loss dominate over OBS loss for a long range of loss probabilities. RTT explains this behaviour

Fig.4 illustrates the way the RTT grows as the WLAN packet dropping probability does, but this does not happen with the OBS packet dropping probability. This is due to the fact that the OBS dropping probability increases with background traffic

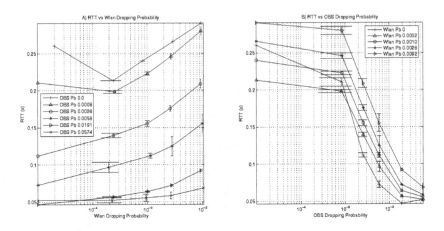

Fig. 4. Mean RTT Graphic in the OBS scenario

load. Consequently, the maximum burst size is reached earlier on average and the RTT decreases. Dropped packets cause a reduction of the Window of TCP, but in OBS this effect is somewhat compensated by a reduction on RTT. Considering that in TCP $Throughput \approx WindowSize/RTT$, the reduction of the RTT softens the effect of the decrement of Window Size and the performance is sustained until the OBS dropping probability is larger than $5 \cdot 10^{-3}$.

6   Conclusions

The presented simulation-based study gives a first understanding of the factors that rule TCP behaviour in a scenario with an OBS core and 802.11 access network. The results show that the throughput achieved, whose maximum is determined by the wireless segment bottleneck, depends heavily on the WLAN dropping probability. The throughput decay is made heavier by the RTT increase caused by retransmissions. The packet loss probability of OBS could approximately be added to this value, given the low drop probabilities considered and the fact that both losses can be assumed independent.

The simulation confirms this fact and provides additional information on how the throughput behaves for the same drop probability at each segment: in a wide range of values, the throughput is dominated by WLAN loss. In the case of WLAN, the RTT grows because of Layer-2 retransmissions, whereas in OBS high drop probabilities are due to high loads, and in these circumstances the RTT shrinks because bursts are sent as soon as the maximum burst size is reached at the edge routers.

As a general consequence, it can be stated that access and core networks can be designed in a largely independent way as long as TCP performance is concerned; the configuration parameters can be selected separately. Furthermore, since TCP is more sensitive to WLAN loss than to OBS loss, more emphasis should be set on improving communication reliability in the radio access than on the core, provided that the OBS network is designed to work far from the throughput-fall point for the carried traffic.

Acknowledgements

This work has been partly supported by the EU under the IST e-Photon/One+ project (FP6-IST-027497) and by the Spanish CAPITAL project (TEC2004-05622-C04-03).

References

1. Chen, Y., Qiao, C., Yu, X.: Optical burst switching: a new area in optical networking research. Network, IEEE 18(3), 16–23 (2004)
2. Kumar, A.: Comparative performance analysis of versions of TCP in a local network with a lossy link. IEEE/ACM Transactions on Networking 6(4), 485–498 (1998)
3. Xylomenos, G., Polyzos, G.C.: TCP and UDP performance over a wireless LAN. INFO-COM 2, 439–446 (1999)
4. Postel, J.: Transmission Control Protocol. RFC 793 (Standard) (September 1981)
5. Allman, M., Paxson, V., Stevens, W.: TCP Congestion Control. RFC 2581 (April 1999)
6. Allman, M., Floyd, S., Partridge, C.: Increasing TCP's Initial Window. RFC 3390 (October 2002)
7. Banchs, A., Perez, X.: Providing throughput guarantees in IEEE 802.11 wireless LAN. In: IEEE Wireless Communications and Networking Conference, 2002 (WCNC 2002), March 2002, pp. 130–138. IEEE Computer Society Press, Los Alamitos (2002)
8. Banchs, A., Perez, X.: Assured and expedited forwarding extensions for IEEE 802.11 Wireless LAN. In: Quality of Service. Tenth IEEE International Workshop, May 2002, vol. 237–246, pp. 237–246. IEEE Computer Society Press, Los Alamitos (2002)
9. Spatscheck, O., Hansen, J.S., Hartman, J.H., Peterson, L.L.: Optimizing TCP forwarder performance. IEEE/ACM Transactions on Networking 8(2), 146–157 (2000)
10. Bhandarkar, S., Sadry, N., Reedy, A., Vaidya, N.: TCP-DCR: A novel protocol for tolerating wireless chaneel errors. IEEE Transactions on Mobile Computing 4(5) (October 2005)
11. Xiong, Y., Vandenhoute, M., Cankaya, H.C.: Control architecture in optical burst-switched WDM networks. Selected Areas in Communications, IEEE Journal on 18(10), 1838–1851 (2000)
12. Gowda, S., Shenai, R., Sivalingam, K., Cankaya, H.: Performance evaluation of TCP over optical burst-switched (OBS) wdm networks. In: Communications, ICC '03, IEEE International Conference, May 2003, pp. 11–15. IEEE Computer Society Press, Los Alamitos (2003)
13. Yu, X., Liu, C.Q.Y.: TCP implementations and false time out detection in obs networks. INFOCOM 2004, 774–784 (March 2004)
14. Ns-2 network simulator: http://www.isi.edu/nsnam/ns/
15. Rappaport, T.S.: Wireless communications, principles and practice. Prentice-Hall, Englewood Cliffs (1996)
16. Chakraborty, D., Ashir, A., Suganuma, T., Keeni, G.M., Roy, T.K., Shiratori, N.: Self-similar and fractal nature of internet traffic. Int. J. Netw. Manag. 14(2), 119–129 (2004)
17. Medina, A., Allman, M., Floyd, S.: Measuring the evolution of transport protocols in the Internet. SIGCOMM Comput. Commun. Rev. 35(2), 37–52 (2005)

Towards Policy-Supported Adaptable Service Systems

Paramai Supadulchai, Finn Arve Aagesen, and Patcharee Thongtra

Department of Telematics
Norwegian University of Science and Technology (NTNU)
N7491 Trondheim, Norway
`paramai@item.ntnu.no, finnarve@item.ntnu.no, patt@item.ntnu.no`

Abstract. This paper presents a policy-supported architecture for adaptable service systems based on the combination of Reasoning Machines and Extended Finite State Machines. Policies are introduced to obtain flexibility with respect to specification and execution of adaptation mechanisms. The presented architecture covers two aspects: service system framework and adaptation mechanisms. The service system framework is a general framework for capability management. Adaptation mechanisms are needed for autonomous adaptation. The adaptation mechanisms can be based on static or dynamic policy systems. Capability management for of a simple music video-on demand service system with runtime simulation results based on the proposed architecture is presented.

1 Introduction

Networked service systems are considered. *Services* are realized by *service components*, which by their inter-working provide a service in the role of a *service provider* to a *service use*r. Service components are executed as software components in *nodes*, which are physical processing units such as servers, routers, switches and user terminals.

An adaptable service system is here defined as a service system which is able to adapt dynamically to changes in time and position related to users, nodes, capabilities, system performance, changed service requirements and policies. In this context, *capability* is defined as an inherent physical *property* of a node, which is used as a basis to implement services. Capabilities can be classified into *resources*, *functions* and *data*. Examples are CPU, memory, transmission capacity of connected transmission links, available special hardware, and available programs and data.

The software mechanisms used for implementing the functionality of the service components of adaptable service systems must be flexible and powerful. Service components based on the classical EFSM (Extended Finite State Machine) approach can be flexibly executed by using generic EFSM executing software components that are able to download and execute different EFSM-based specifications [1].

In addition to this type of flexibility the *EFSM-based* functionality can be supplemented by *reasoning-machine* (RM) based functionality, which makes policy-based specification and operation possible. *"Policies represent externalized logic that can determine the behavior of the managed systems"* [2]. In this paper *a policy is technically defined as a set of rules with related actions.* A *policy system* is a set of policies,

A. Pras and M. van Sinderen (Eds.): EUNICE 2007, LNCS 4606, pp. 128–140, 2007.

and an *RM-based functionality is using a policy system to manage the behavior of a target system, which can be* another policy system. A *static policy system* has a non changeable set of rules and actions, while a *dynamic policy* system has a changeable set of rules and actions.

Policy-based software has a specification style, which is expressive and flexible. Software functionality based on policy-based specifications, however, also needs to be appropriately specified and validated. The validation aspect is outside the scope of this paper.

The main contribution of this paper is the presentation of a generic service framework for adaptable service systems that combines the use of EFSM-based and RM-based service components. In this context the reasoning machines can be used

a)   as ordinary procedural services for EFSM-based service components
b)   for instantiation and re-instantiation (i.e. after movement) of   EFSM-based service components according to the availability and need of capabilities
c)   to adapt the behavior of and capabilities allocated to instantiated EFSM-based service components in the nodes where they are instantiated

This paper has focus on issue c), but the framework presented can be used for a) and b) also. In general, adaptation needs appropriate mechanisms to guarantee the wanted results. For autonomous adaptation stable feedback loops [3], which control the performance, are needed. As the capabilities are limited, the access to the system must be controlled, and there must also be priority mechanisms that give priority to users which are willing to pay more and/or are in a higher need in situations with lack of capabilities.

The issues of policy-supported adaptable service system architecture are in this paper classified into 3 main aspects: A) Service system framework, B) Adaptation mechanism and C) Data model. *Service system framework* comprises abstraction, concepts and models. *Adaptation mechanism* concerns the use of the appropriate policies to control the service system when it is entering a state where RM functionality is needed. *Data model* concerns the data representation of the service system framework and adaptation mechanisms.

This paper comprises the aspects A) and B) only. For details about the data model, which is based on XML Equivalent Transformation language (*XET*), Common Information Model (CIM) and Resource Definition Framework (RDF), the reader is referred to [1] and [4]. The remaining part of this paper is structured as follows. Section 2 discusses related work. Section 3 presents the service system framework. Section 4 presents policy-based adaptation mechanism. Section 5 presents the models and results for example application cases related to capability management of a music video on-demand service. Section 6 gives summary and conclusions.

2   Related Work

Most of recent works related to policy-based adaptable service systems focus on the aspects A) and B) as defined in Section 1. Examples are [2, 5-10]. The aspect C) is supported by XML-based language in [2, 10], which is analogous to our used XML

Equivalent Transformation (XET). However, [2] has a weak focus on the aspects A) and B), while [10] has a weak focus on A).

Considering the nature of the policies, [5] is preliminary aimed at static policies, while [6-10] are both using static and dynamic policies. Excluding [8], systems capable of dynamic policies [6-7, 9, 10] are based on proper feedbacks. The feedback loops in [5, 7, 9, 10] are used to evaluate the service system rather than policies. The loop in [6] evaluates policies. However, the evaluation is based on complex mathematical equations and not by additional policy sets.

The adaptation mechanisms presented in this paper can use static as well as dynamic policies. Considering the dynamic policy, the rule-based modification of the policy managing the service system can be composed at run-time.

The use of dynamic policies in [9, 10] as well as in this paper also aims at being a flexible tool for the experimentation with alternative policies with respect to optimization.

3 Service System Framework

The concept *capability* was defined in Section 1. *Capability performance measures* are the concepts used for the performance modeling, dimensioning, analyzing, monitoring and management of capabilities. Capability performance measures comprise capability *capacity*, capability *state* and capability *Quality of Service* (QoS) measures (e.g. traffic and availability measures). *Service performance measures* are performance measures related to the service provided to the service user (e.g. QoS measures) as well as service system state measures.

An executing service system consists of executing service components which are *instances* of *service component type*s. The functionality types are *EFSM types* and *RM types*. The basic functionality of the service components, however, are based on EFSMs supported and/or controlled by RMs. EFSM components will have requirements with respect to *capability* and *service performance* to be able to perform their intended functionality (Fig. 1). These requirements are denoted as required capability and service performance. The capability and service performance of an executing service system are denoted as inherent capability and service performance.

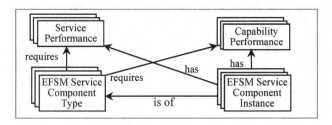

Fig. 1. EFSM part of Service System – Concept Structure

Capability management (CM) is an important function within an adaptable service system and comprises: 1) service system capability initialization, 2) capability allocation adaptation and 3) capability re-initialization. *Service system capability initialization* is the allocation of the capabilities for the service components to be distributed and instantiated. Capabilities are allocated according to the system performance requirements of the EFSM components of a service system. *Capability allocation adaptation* is the monitoring of the performance of the executing service system and the reallocation of capabilities within the executing service systems. In situations when the instantiated service systems are unable to adapt satisfactory, capability management can initiate a *service system capability re-initialization* for a re-distribution and re-instantiation of the service system.

As a basis for the optimal adaptation, *service level agreements* (SLA) are needed between the *service users* and the *service provider*. The service provider view of this service level agreement can in this context be considered as a part of executing service components. A number of QoS levels can exist. The agreement can contain elements such as: agreed QoS levels, required capabilities, required system performance, payment for the service in case of agreed QoS level and payments for the service in case of reduced QoS level. A service level agreement class (SLA class) defines provided service user functionalities as well as agreed QoS parameter and cost values for a group of service users with different degree of satisfactions and cost.

In the following a formalized service framework model is presented. The following concepts are defined:

E	Functionality set of an EFSM type	$\hat{C}_A$	Set of available capabilities in nodes
$\hat{E}$	Functionality set of an EFSM instance	S	Service performance measures set
$\mathcal{R}$	Functionality set of a RM type	$\hat{S}_R$	Required service performance set for an EFSM-based service component type
$\hat{\mathcal{R}}$	Functionality set of a RM instance		
C	Capability performance measures set	$\hat{S}_I$	Inherent service performance set of an executing EFSM-based service component
$\hat{C}_R$	Required capability performance set for an EFSM-based service component type		
$\hat{C}_I$	Inherent capability performance set of an executing EFSM-based service component	I	Income functions set for the service components constituting a service. These functions will depend on the system performance.

The EFSM type E and the RM type $\mathcal{R}$ are defined ($\equiv$) as follows:

$$E \quad \equiv \quad \{ \, S_M, S_I, V, P, M(P), O(P), F_S, F_O, F_V \, \} \tag{1}$$

$$\mathcal{R} \quad \equiv \quad \{ \, \mathcal{Q}, \mathcal{F}, \mathcal{P}, \mathcal{T}, \mathcal{E}, \Sigma \, \} \tag{2a}$$

$$\mathcal{P} \quad \equiv \quad \{ \, \mathcal{X}, \mathcal{A} \, \} \tag{2b}$$

Concerning E, S_M is the set of states, S_I is the initial state, V is a set of variables, P is a set of parameters, $M(P)$ is a set of input signal with parameters, $O(P)$ is a set of output signal with parameters, F_S is the state transition function ($F_S = S \times M(P) \times V$), F_O is the output function, ($F_O = S \times M(P) \times V$) and F_V are the functions and tasks performed during a specific state transition such as computation on local data, communication initialization, database access, etc.

Concerning $\mathcal{R}$ and $\mathcal{P}$, $\mathcal{Q}$ is the set of messages, $\mathcal{F}$ is a generic *reasoning procedure*, $\mathcal{P}$ is a policy system which consists of a set of rules $\mathcal{X}$ and a set of actions $\mathcal{A}$, $\mathcal{T}$ is a set of *system constraints* and $\mathcal{E}$ is a set of *performance data*. The *reasoning procedure* is the procedure applied by RM to select the appropriate actions. The performance data represents the inherent performance of the targeted system. The system constraints represent the variables of the system and the defined constraints and relationships between variables. The policy rules are based on the variables of the constraints. Σ is a set of reasoning conditions defined by *trigger conditions* Σ_T, *and goal conditions* Σ_G. RM functionality is activated when a Σ_T is detected until a Σ_G is reached. When a trigger condition is true, the reasoning procedure transforms Q_i to Q_j by using P to match the system constraints T against the *performance data* $\mathcal{E}$ and a set of suggest actions $\{\mathcal{A}_i, \mathcal{A}_j, \mathcal{A}_k...\} \subseteq \mathcal{A}$. These actions may also set the next state and values of the variables of EFSM-based service component instances. The *reasoning procedure* is based on *Equivalent Transformation* (*ET*) [11], which solves a given problem by transforming it through repetitive application of (semantically) equivalent transformation rules.

The RM functionality will need EFSM support for the continuous updating of T, $\mathcal{E}$ and Σ, and for the activation and deactivation of the reasoning machines. This is done by EFSMs, and in this case T, $\mathcal{E}$ and Σ are considered as common data for the EFSMs and the associated RM-based functionality. A dedicated EFSM E_Σ has the duty to inspect the reasoning condition and to activate and to deactivate the reasoning machine.

4 Policy-Based Adaptation Mechanism

4.1 System Constraints, Performance Data and Reasoning Conditions

The elements T and $\mathcal{E}$ of an RM as defined in Section 3 depend on the structuring and the nature of the reasoning functionality. A *reasoning cluster, which* is an independent unit with respect to reasoning, is a collection of EFSM-based service components with an associated *reasoning system* constituted by one or more *reasoning machine*s. A reasoning cluster has a set of associated income functions I. The elements T and $\mathcal{E}$ of a reasoning cluster with available capabilities from N_{Node} nodes, consisting of K EFSM-based service component types and L_k instances of an EFSM-based service type k are defined as follows:

$$T \quad \equiv \quad Expr\ \{S, C, I, (E_k, \hat{S}_{R,k}, \hat{C}_{R,k}; k = [1, K])\} \tag{3}$$

$$\mathcal{E} \quad \equiv \quad \{((\hat{E}_{lk}, \hat{S}_{I,lk}, \hat{C}_{I,lk}; l = [1, L_k]), k = [1, K]), \tag{4}$$

$$(\hat{C}_{A,n}; n = [1, N_{Node}])\}$$

The function $Expr\{X_i; i = [1, I]\}$ in (3) symbolizes the set $\{X_i; i = [1, I]\}$ and also some set of logical functions based on the elements of the set. The system constraints T related to a reasoning cluster comprise the EFSM functionality sets of the EFSM-based service component types, required capability and service performance, as well as the income functions for the reasoning cluster. The performance data $\mathcal{E}$ defined in (4) is a set of the inherent capability and service performance for all instances of EFSM-based service components in the reasoning cluster, as well as available capabilities of the nodes that potentially can contribute their capabilities for the EFSM-based functionality of the reasoning cluster.

The components constituting the *reasoning condition* Σ are the states and variables of the EFSM-based service component types, and the capability and service performance measures C and S as given in (5).

$$\Sigma \quad \equiv \quad Expr \: \{S, \: C, \: (\: E_k, \hat{S}_{R,k}, \hat{C}_{R,k} \: ; \: k = [1, \: K]) \} \tag{5}$$

Capability Management (CM) as defined in Section 3 goes beyond the boundaries of an individual reasoning cluster as well as an individual service system. This means that CM in general must be handled by a common distributed algorithm or by a centralized reasoning cluster.

4.2 Policy-Based Adaptation Using Static Policies

The adaptation mechanism using static policies is illustrated in Fig. 2. The rules $\mathcal{X}$ are unchangeable. When the service systems enter a Σ_T, Service System Adaptation Manager ($\mathcal{R}_1$) is activated and tries to lead the system back to a goal state Σ_G. $\mathcal{R}_1$ is deactivated when service systems enter Σ_G.

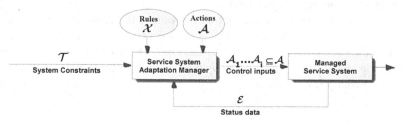

Fig. 2. Policy-based adaptation using static policies

4.3 Policy-Based Adaptation Using Dynamic Policies

The adaptation mechanism using dynamic policies is illustrated in Fig. 3. In addition to the Service System Adaptation Manager ($\mathcal{R}_1$) a Policy Evaluator ($\mathcal{R}_2$) is used.

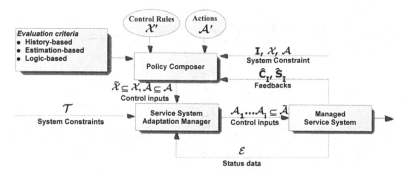

Fig. 3. Policy based adaptation based on dynamic policies

A generic rule-based reasoning system with dynamic policy can be defined by (6a, 6b, 6c and 6d) as follows:

$$\mathcal{R}_1 \equiv \{ \mathcal{Q}, \mathcal{F}, \tilde{\mathcal{P}}, \mathcal{T}, \mathcal{E}, \Sigma \} \tag{6a}$$

$$\tilde{\mathcal{P}} \equiv \{ \tilde{\mathcal{X}}, \tilde{\mathcal{A}} \} \tag{6b}$$

$$\mathcal{R}_2 \equiv \{ \mathcal{Q}', \mathcal{F}, \mathcal{P}', \mathcal{T}', \mathcal{E}', \Sigma' \} \tag{6c}$$

$$\mathcal{P}' \equiv \{ \mathcal{X}', \mathcal{A}' \} \tag{6d}$$

where $\mathcal{T}' = \{I, \mathcal{X}, \mathcal{A}\}$ and $\mathcal{E}' = \{ \hat{C}_I, \hat{S}_I \}$. $\mathcal{Q}'$ is a set of messages between $\hat{\mathcal{R}}_1$ and $\mathcal{R}_2$. $\mathcal{X}$ is a set of control rules that can re-order the priority of the rules, activate and de-activate the rules and change rules' constraints. The policy evaluator evaluates the system policy at runtime based on *evaluation criteria, reference inputs* and *feedbacks*. Income functions are used as reference inputs, while the feedbacks are system performance measures. Evaluation criteria can in general be history-based and prediction-based. This paper is only using history-based evaluation, which determines the consequences of the rules in the past using service performance measures. The prediction-based evaluation determines the consequences of rules in the future based on mathematical equations represented by $\mathcal{X}'$.

Dynamic policies need a certain period to evaluate the consequences of the rules used. A measure for *the learning ability* is the *learning time* (T_L), which is the time needed by the system to properly evaluate the rules. The *learning time* T_L depends on the service performance measures used by the evaluation algorithm. However, there is no unique and easy way to define T_L.

5   Application Examples

5.1   The Application Cases

Five application cases (Case I-V) for a simple service system handling the capability management for a music video on-demand service is presented. The intention is to illustrate the use of the proposed policy-based service system architecture, and the

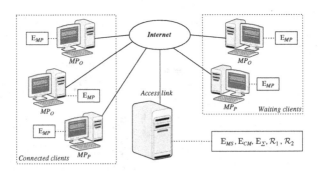

Fig. 4. A music video on-demand service system; E_{MS}: Media server type, E_{MP}: Media player type, E_{CM}: Capability manager type, E_Σ: Dedicated EFSM type for controlling the reasoning mechanism, $\mathcal{R}_1$: Service system adaptation manager type, $\mathcal{R}_2$: Policy evaluator type

potential advantages of using dynamic policies. The Cases I - III use no policy, Case IV uses static policies, while Case V uses dynamic policies. The service system is constituted by one or more media servers (MS) streaming media files to media players (MP) (Fig. 4). The numbers of MS used in Case I, II and III are fixed (one, two and three respectively), while the number in Case IV and V can vary from one to three.

The basic EFSM types constituting the capability management system are media server handler (E_{MS}), media player handler (E_{MP}) and capability manager (E_{CM})

The capability manager, which operation is based on policy based adaptation, is used in Case IV and V. According to the definition of capability management in Section 3, service system capability initialization and re-initialization is not included in the example. This means that only capability allocation adaptation is considered. With reference to the concepts service system adaptation manger and policy evaluator as defined in Section 4, the capability manager now has the role of a service system adaptation manager, and the policy evaluator is the system determining the policies to be used of the capability manager.

In the fixed policy case (Case IV) E_{CM} is supported by a rule-based reasoning system $\mathcal{R}_1$, and in the dynamic policy case (Case V) E_{CM} is supported by $\mathcal{R}_1$ and $\mathcal{R}_2$. The EFSM type E_Σ is the dedicated EFSM that inspects the reasoning conditions Σ and activates/deactivates the reasoning mechanisms.

The MS's required access link capacity $C_{R,AL}$ is set to 100 Mbps. The number of MPs that can use the service is limited by the MS access link capacity. An MP belongs to a *SLA_Class*. In the example two classes are applied: premium (MP_P) and ordinary (MP_O). Three different streaming throughput bit-rates (X) are offered, 500Kbps, 600 Kbps and 1Mbps. MP_O connections are 500Kbps (X_O) while MP_P connections can be either 600Kbps or 1Mbps (X_P).

The service level agreements comprise *required streaming throughput, maximum waiting time, payment for the service* and *penalties for not satisfying the service*. The required streaming throughput of MP_O and MP_P are X_O and $X_{P,}$ respectively.

The mechanisms used by the capability manager are to let client wait, to disconnect ordinary clients, to decrease the throughput of the premium clients and to change the number of media servers.

When the required streaming throughput cannot be provided, an MP may have to wait until some connected MPs have finished using the service. This will result in money payback to the waiting MPs. An MP_O can be disconnected, while an MP_P may have to reduce the throughput. If a client is disconnected, the service provider pays a penalty. The maximum waiting time for MP_P and MP_O are 60 seconds and infinite respectively.

The service performance measures $\hat{S}_I$ are the number of connected and waiting premium and ordinary clients ($N_{Con,P}$, $N_{Con,O}$, $N_{Wait,P}$, $N_{Wait,O}$), the number of disconnected MP_O ($N_{Dis,O}$), the number of MS (N_{MS}), inherent streaming throughput (X_I), the number of available nodes (N_{Node}) and the accumulated service time and waiting time of premium and ordinary clients ($T_{Serv,P}$, $T_{Serv,O}$, $T_{Wait,P}$, $T_{Wait,O}$). These values are observed per monitoring interval Δ.

A *unit* is the price paid by an ordinary customer for *one second streaming* of the rate 500 Kbps. The income function for the service provider is m(SLA_Class, X_I) (units/s). The penalty function for waiting is p_{Wait}(SLA_Class) (units/s). The penalty function for disconnections is p_{Dis}(SLA_Class) (units/disconnection). The cost function for adding a new server is p_{Ser} (units/s per Node). The total income function (m_T) during the monitoring interval Δ is:

$$m_T = m(MP_O, X_{I,O}) \times T_{Serv,O} + m(MP_P, X_{I,P}) \times T_{Serv,P} - p_{Wait}(MP_O) \times T_{Wait,O}$$

$$- p_{Wait}(MP_P) \times T_{Wait,P} - p_{Dis}(MP_O) \times N_{Dis,O} \quad - p_{Ser} \times (N_{MS^-}) \times \Delta \quad (7)$$

The reasoning machine supported capability manager will try to maximize the total income. The service system is realized as one reasoning cluster as illustrated in Fig. 4. The nature of the *service system adaptation manager* as well as the need and nature of a *policy evaluator* depends on the difference in income and penalty for the different SLA classes, as well as the cost for introducing a new server. If the income and penalty for premium service class is relatively higher than for an ordinary class, it can be profitable to disconnect some MP_O and let some MP_P get the service instead.

The specification of the behavior of the *service system adaptation manager* used for the Cases IV and V, and the *policy evaluator* applied for the Case V is given in Appendix.

5.2   Results

The MP arrivals are modeled as a Poisson process with parameter λ_{SLA_Class}. The duration of streaming connections d_{SLA_Class} is constant. The quantity $\rho = ((\lambda_O \times d_O \times X_O) + (\lambda_P \times d_P \times X_P))/C_{I,AL}$ is the traffic per an MS access link. Intuitively, the system with $\rho \leq 1$ needs at least one server while the system with $1 \leq \rho \leq 2$ needs at least two servers and so on. The MP_P arrival intensity is 15% of the total arrival intensity. The duration of streaming connections are set to 10 minutes, while the monitoring interval Δ is set to 1 minute. MPs stop waiting after 10 minutes. The income and penalty functions in units are given in Table 1. The cost for using an extra MS is 833 units/s per Node.

Table 1. Income and penalty functions

	MP_O	MP_P (X_I = 600Kbps)	MP_P (X_I = 1Mbps)
m(SLA_Class, X_I) / s	1	1.875	2
p_{Wait}(SLA_Class) / s	5	10	10
p_{Dis}(SLA_Class) / disconnection	10	-	-

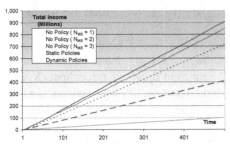

Fig. 5. Accumulated total income for $\rho = 3.45$

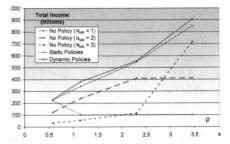

Fig. 6. Accumulated income at 500th ms

Fig. 5 illustrates the accumulated total income when ρ = 3.45. The value 3.45 is chosen to compare the no-policy scenarios with N_{MS} = 1, 2, or 3 and as well as the static and dynamic policy scenarios. The accumulated total incomes of cases with no policy are relatively lower than those with policies.

Fig. 6 illustrates the values of accumulated total income at the 500th minute for the ρ values: 0.56, 1,2, 2.3 and 3.5. The systems with no policy produce good results with a certain load region. The systems operated under policies produced higher accumulated total income independent of load region. Dynamic policies give relatively better result. These cases also have the potential improvement by changing the policies.

Fig. 7 shows the system behavior for Case IV and V when the traffic is being increased or decreased (the value of ρ varies as a function of time). The time with ρ at a fixed level is denoted as the ρ *period*. The dotted line shows the variation of ρ, which can take the values 0.5, 1, 1.5 and 2 times of ρ = 1.44. The ρ period, which is $10 \times d_{SLA\_Class}$, provides much time for the system for learning the consequences of the rules being applied. Case V gives a better result.

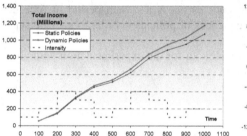

Fig. 7. Accumulated total income

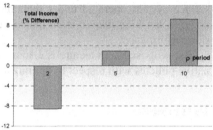

Fig. 8. Comparison of Case IV&V

Fig. 8 shows a comparison between Case IV and V for different ρ periods. The figure shows the difference between the values of accumulated total income after 500 minutes. When the ρ period is small, Case IV may give better result because the system need more learning time (T_L). The T_L value falls between $2 \times$ and $5 \times d_{SLA\_Class}$.

The use of $\mathcal{X}_3$, $\mathcal{X}_4$ (see Appendix), which will add or remove an MS, affects the system's accumulated total income. Having more MS all the time is better for high traffic while having few MS all the time is better for low traffic. The policy evaluator learned this by observing the consequences of $\mathcal{X}_3$ and $\mathcal{X}_4$. The ability to learn can also be improved by appropriately selecting service performance measures and algorithms.

6   Conclusion

An architecture for policy-based adaptable service systems, based on the combination of Reasoning Machines (RMs) and Extended Finite State Machines (EFSMs) has been presented. Policies have been introduced with the intension to increase flexibility in the system specification and execution.

The adaptation mechanism uses policies to control service systems when it is entering a reasoning condition. The use of policy can be of two types: *static* or *dynamic*. In the static case the reasoning system *constituted by a service system adaptation manager* determines a list of suggested actions that will control the behavior of the service system. In the dynamic case an additional RM, denoted as the *policy evaluator*, is added. The *policy evaluator* is able to compose policy on-the-fly, and has the ability to estimate or evaluate the consequences of the rules of a policy based on their accumulated goodness scores.

Five application cases handling the capability management of a music video on-demand service are presented. The intention is to illustrate the use of the proposed architecture and demonstrate the potential advantage of using dynamic policies. Case I, II and III use no policies. Case IV uses static policies, while Case V uses dynamic policies. Only capability allocation adaptation is considered. There are situations where the use of no policy can be superior or equal to the use of policies. The selected system parameters can represent an optimal dimensioning. However, the same set of system parameters will likely not be optimal for other system traffic load cases. The service system operated under static policies give a relatively high income in both low and high traffic. The service system operated under dynamic policies, however, has a performance which is superior or equal to other application cases. Nevertheless, the service system operated under dynamic policies needs a certain period of time denoted as *learning time* to learn the consequences of policies in order to provide superior performance.

The proposed architecture is also a flexible tool for the experimentation with alternative policies with respect to optimization.

References

1. Aagesen, F.A., Supadulchai, P., Anutariya, C., Shiaa, M.M.: Configuration Management for an Adaptable Service System. In: IFIP International Conference on Metropolitan Area Networks, Architecture, Protocols, Control, and Management, Ho Chi Minh City, Viet Nam (2005)
2. Agrawal, D., Lee, K.-W., Lobo, J.: Policy-Based Management of Networked Computing Systems. IEEE Communications Magazine 43, 69–75 (2005)
3. Diao, Y., Hellerstein, J.L., Parekh, S., Griffith, R., Kaiser, G., Phung, D.: A Control Theory Foundation for Self-Managing Computing Systems. IEEE Journal on Selected Areas in Communications 23, 2213–2222 (2005)
4. Supadulchai, P., Aagesen, F.A.: A Framework for Dynamic Service Composition. In: First International IEEE Workshop on Autonomic Communications and Computing (ACC 2005), Taormina, Italy, IEEE Computer Society Press, Los Alamitos (2005)
5. Garlan, D., Cheng, S.-W., Huang, A.-C., Schmerl, B., Steenkiste, P.: Rainbow: Architecture-Based Self-Adaptation with Reusable Instrastructure. Computer 37, 46–54 (2004)
6. Samaan, N., Karmouch, A.: An Automated Policy-Based Management Framework for Differentiated Communication Systems. IEEE Journal on Selected Areas in Communications 23, 2236–2247 (2005)
7. Nasri, R., Altman, Z., Dubreil, H.: Autonomic Mobile Network Management Techniques for Self-Parameterisation and Auto-regulation. In: Smartnet 2006, Paris (2006)
8. Kanada, Y.: Dynamically Extensible Policy Server and Agent. In: Proceedings of the 3rd Int'l Workshop on Policies for Distributed Systems and Networks (POLICY'02) (2002)

9. Chan, H., Kwok, T.: A Policy-based Management System with Automatic Policy Selection and Creation Capabilities using a Singular Value Decomposition Technique. In: Proceedings of the 7th IEEE International Workshop on Policies for Distributed Systems and Networks (POLICY'06), IEEE Computer Society Press, Los Alamitos (2006)
10. Anthony, R.J.: A Policy-Definition Language and Prototype Implementation Library for Policy-based Autonomic Systems. In: Autonomic Computing, ICAC '06. IEEE International Conference, IEEE Computer Society Press, Los Alamitos (2006)
11. Akama, K., Shimitsu, T., Miyamoto, E.: Solving Problems by Equivalent Transformation of Declarative Programs. Journal of the Japanese Society of Artificial Intelligence 13, 944–952 (1998)

Appendix. Reasoning Machine Specifications

1 Service System Adaptation Manager (Case IV and V)

The set of actions $\mathcal{A}$ applied by the service system adaptation manger is:

$$\mathcal{A} \quad \equiv \quad \{ \mathcal{A}_D, \mathcal{A}_B, \mathcal{A}_I, \mathcal{A}_R \} \tag{A.1}$$

$\mathcal{A}_D$ *(Disconnect-Client)* tells MS to disconnect suggested MP_O. $\mathcal{A}_B$ *(Decrease-Bit-Rate)* tells MS to reduce throughput of suggested MP_P for a certain time period. $\mathcal{A}_I$ *(Initialize-Server)* tells MS to initiate a new MS, while $\mathcal{A}_R$ *(Remove-Server)* will remove a MS. Concerning the reasoning condition set $\Sigma \equiv \{ \Sigma_{T1}, \Sigma_{G1} \}$, the reasoning activation condition Σ_{T1} is $N_{Wait,P} + N_{Wait,O} > 0$ and the reasoning goal condition Σ_{G1} is $N_{Wait,P} + N_{Wait,O} = 0$. The rule set $\mathcal{X}$ for the service system adaptation manger is:

$$\mathcal{X} \quad \equiv \quad \{ \mathcal{X}_1, \mathcal{X}_2, \mathcal{X}_3, \mathcal{X}_4 \} \tag{A.2}$$

$\mathcal{X}_1$ suggests $\mathcal{A}_D$ for disconnecting a list of suggested MP_O when $p_{Wait}(MP_O) < p_{Wait}(MP_P)$. The number of MP_O is calculated from $N_{Wait,P} \times X_{P,1Mbps} / X_O$. $\mathcal{X}_2$ suggests $\mathcal{A}_B$ for reducing throughput of a list of suggested MP_P when $p_{Wait}(MP_O) > m(MP_P, X_{P,1Mbps}) - m(MP_P, X_{P,600Kbps})$. The number of MP_P to decrease bandwidth is calculated from $N_{Wait,O} \times X_O / (X_{P,1Mbps} - X_{P,600Kbps})$. $\mathcal{X}_3$ suggests $\mathcal{A}_I$ for initiating a new MS when $X_P \times N_{Wait,P} + X_O \times N_{Wait,O} / C_{R,AL} > 0.1$. $\mathcal{X}_4$ suggests $\mathcal{A}_R$ for removing an MS when $X_P \times N_{Wait,P} + X_O \times N_{Wait,O} / C_{R,AL} < 0.1$.

2 Policy Evaluator (Case V)

The policy evaluator will be activated and de-activated whenever the service system adaptation manager is activated and de-activated. So we have activation condition $\Sigma_{T2} \doteq \Sigma_{T1}$ ($\doteq$ means *'is instantiated as'*), and goal condition $\Sigma_{G2} \doteq \Sigma_{G1}$. The set of actions $\mathcal{A}$ applied by the the policy evaluator is:

$$\mathcal{A}' \quad \equiv \quad \{ \mathcal{A}_G(\mathcal{X}_i), \mathcal{A}_T(\mathcal{X}_i) \} \tag{A.3}$$

$\mathcal{A}_G(\mathcal{X}_i)$ is an action for the calculate of the *accumulated goodness score* of a rule $\mathcal{X}_i$. $\mathcal{A}_T(\mathcal{X}_i)$ is an action to suspend $\mathcal{X}_I$ for a certain time period. The *goodness score of a rule* $(Qo\mathcal{X}_i)$ during the monitoring time interval T is calculated by the percentage of the increased or decreased total income (m_T). The algorithm to calculate $Qo\mathcal{X}_i$ is as follows:

$$Qo\mathcal{X}_I \quad = \quad Qo\mathcal{X}_i + \frac{m_{T,t} - m_{T,t-1}}{m_{T,t}} \times 100 \tag{A.4}$$

where $m_{T,t}$ and $m_{T,t-1}$ are the total income during the current and previous monitoring interval respectively. The rule set $\mathcal{X}$ of the policy evaluator is:

$$\mathcal{X} \quad \equiv \quad \{ \mathcal{X}_1, \mathcal{X}_2 \} \tag{A.5}$$

$\mathcal{X}_1$ calculate the goodness score of the rule used during the last interval using the action $\mathcal{A}_G(\mathcal{X}_i)$, and $\mathcal{X}_2$ suspends rules using the action $\mathcal{A}_T(\mathcal{X}_i)$ when their goodness scores are below zero.

An Architecture for the Self-management of Lambda-Connections in Hybrid Networks

Tiago Fioreze, Remco van de Meent, and Aiko Pras

University of Twente, Enschede, the Netherlands
{t.fioreze, r.vandemeent, a.pras}@utwente.nl

Abstract. Hybrid networks are networks capable of switching data at multiple levels (optical and IP packet level) by means of multi-service optical switches. As a result of that, huge flows at the IP-level may be moved to the optical-level, which is faster than the packet-level. Such move could be beneficial since congested IP networks could be off-loaded, leaving more resources for other IP flows. At the same time, the flows switched at the optical-level would get better Quality of Service (QoS). In order to achieve this beneficial move, huge IP flows have to be properly detected at the packet-level and lambda-connections are to be established for them at the optical-level. Two approaches are currently used for that purpose: the first is based on conventional management techniques and the second is based on GMPLS signaling. Both approaches mostly depend on human intervention, which can be error prone and slow. The idea proposed in this paper to overcome this problem consists of adding self-management capabilities to the multi-service optical switches. The optical switches would then be responsible for automatically identifying IP flows, and establishing and releasing lambda-connections for such flows. The main goal of this paper is therefore to propose an architecture for the self-management of lambda-connections in hybrid networks.

1 Introduction

Hybrid networks are networks that allow data to be switched both at the IP packet-level and at the optical-level [1]. An example of a hybrid network is SURFnet6 [2], the Dutch research and education network. Hybrid networks are composed by multi-service optical switches, which have the capability to perform forwarding decisions at different levels in the protocol stack. As a result of that, big and long IP flows (so called elephant flows) could be moved from the packet-level to the optical-level. It is anticipated that such a move results in a better Quality of Service (QoS) for both elephant flows and remaining IP flows at the packet-level: the former would have less delay and jitter and plenty of bandwidth at the optical-level; the latter would be better served due to the off-loading of elephant flows.

An accurate identification of IP flows and a proper management of lambda-connections are important tasks to achieve the desired move. Two approaches are currently used for that [3]: conventional management and GMPLS signaling. The former is characterized by a centralized management entity (e.g., human manager or an automated management process) that is in charge of establishing lambda-connections and deciding which IP flows should be moved to the optical-level. In contrast, the latter

A. Pras and M. van Sinderen (Eds.): EUNICE 2007, LNCS 4606, pp. 141–148, 2007.

is characterized by the fact that optical switches coordinate the creation of lambda-connections among themselves after being triggered for that. The decision which IP flows will be moved to the optical-level however is taken by a centralized entity or by the entities exchanging data flows.

Both approaches, however, have some shortcomings. Both approaches require human interaction to detect flows and manage lambda-connections. This interaction may be slow and error prone. Currently, when a lambda-connection is requested within one single domain (intra-domain), several steps are taken (e.g., phone calls and emails exchanging) between requesters and network domain administrators in order to establish the lambda-connection. Evidently, it may take hours or more before a desired lambda-connection can be used. When the requests for a connection spans multiple domains (inter-domain), the lambda-connection provisioning may take even much longer. In addition to that, a troubleshooting process may be needed to solve connection problems, which may delay the connection setup still more.

Moreover, several big IP flows may, for instance, be using resources at the packet-level while the lambda-connection is being established, and therefore possibly congesting the IP-level. Moreover, by the time that the lambda-connection is finally established the elephant flows may no longer exist or not be large enough for a dedicated lambda-connection.

Our solution to overcome these shortcomings consists of extending the GMPLS approach by automatically detecting IP flows eligible for lambda-connections. With this extension, multi-service optical switches automatically detect IP flows and establish/release lambda-connections for them. This can be characterized as a self-management behavior. In this context, the main goal of this paper is to propose an architecture for the self-management of lambda-connections in hybrid networks.

The remainder of this paper is organized as follows. Section 2 shows the current approaches for the management of lambda-connections. Then, sect. 3 starts by presenting the shortcomings of the current approaches, which have motivated our proposal. In addition, sect. 3 also introduces our architecture for the self-management of lambda-connections. Finally, conclusions and future plans are outlined in sect. 4.

2   Current Management Approaches

This section describes the two current approaches used to manage optical networks: the conventional management approach and the GMPLS signaling approach.

2.1   Conventional Management

The conventional management approach is composed by managers and agents [4]. Managers consist of entities that are responsible for managing the network activity by ordering tasks (e.g., configuration or monitoring actions) for agents. Agents are entities in charge of performing the requested tasks. There may also be entities that can play a dual role, acting as both a manager and an agent.

In the optical networks context a manager can be a centralized management entity (e.g., human manager) that is responsible for managing optical switches (agents) in the optical domain. This centralized management entity is responsible for identifying IP flows to the optical-level and as well the establishment of the optical connections.

The identification of IP flows can be done with the help of monitoring mechanisms, such as NetFlow [5]. On its turn, the establishment of lambda-connections can be performed by using management technologies such as command line interface [6], the well-known SNMP protocol [7] and the TL1 language [8]. When the required lambda-connection spans multiple optical switches, the establishment of the lambda-connection involves setting up each optical switch along the desired path.

2.2 GMPLS Signaling

The Generalized Multiprotocol Label Switching (GMPLS) architecture [9] aims at extending the characteristics of the MPLS architecture [10] to support peculiarities existing in today's optical networks. GMPLS extends MPLS in order to provide to the control plane (signaling and routing) with new label capabilities. GMPLS supports spatial (port), lambda, and time-division switching, besides the traditional packet switching. Unlike in MPLS, however, in the GMPLS architecture the labels are no longer carried in the data, but they are defined in the optical switches.

With regard to the configuration process of the optical switches, GMPLS works similarly to MPLS by using signaling messages in order to establish lambda-connections. On the other hand, regarding to its operational model, GMPLS can be deployed as two different operational models [11]: peer and overlay model.

In the peer model, the topology of the core network is not hidden from users (e.g., adjacent IP networks) of the optical networks, which enables the users to see the entire optical network topology and to choose the desired lambda-connection path. Once the desired path is chosen, the users have to communicate with the most adjacent optical switch by informing it with the desired path, the source and destination addresses of the selected IP flow, and also inform GMPLS signaling parameters (e.g., switching type). Once the adjacent optical switch gets this information, it starts then the process of establishing the desired path by interacting with other switches along the path.

In the overlay model, only the adjacent optical switches are revealed to users of the optical network; topology of the core network is hidden. Hence, users are not able to choose their entire desired connection path. Therefore, to create a lambda-connection, the users can inform their adjacent switch only with the source and destination addresses of the selected IP flow and the GMPLS signaling parameters. The adjacent switch then interacts with other switches to decide which path will be chosen (by using interior gateway protocols such as OSPF or IS-IS) based on the connection parameters provided by the users.

3   The Self-management Architecture

This section presents our architecture for the self-management of lambda-connections in hybrid networks. The section starts by showing some shortcomings of the current approaches and by presenting our idea to overcome them. Then, our proposed architecture is introduced by presenting first its functional part and then its physical part.

3.1   Self-management of Lambda-Connections

The management approaches presented in section 2 have some shortcomings. Both approaches depend on human intervention to select and move IP flows to the optical-level and establish/release lambda-connections. This intervention can be therefore prone to errors and take considerable time to be performed (e.g. weeks).

In the conventional management approach, the network manager has the task of deciding which flows will be moved to the optical-level. This decision is mostly made manually by collecting network information and analyze it. Nonetheless, the network manager has also to configure each optical switch along the chosen path in order to establish lambda-connections for the selected flows. In addition to that, he is required to release the connections when no longer needed as well.

On its turn, the GMPLS signaling approach offers some autonomy in the steps of establishing and releasing lambda-connections. However, these steps must still explicitly be triggered by the users or network managers of the optical network. In addition to that, these users and network managers must also to provide the information about which IP flows will be moved to the optical-level.

Our solution to overcome these shortcomings consists of providing self-management capabilities to optical switches. Our self-management solution allow optical switches to be in charge of automatically selecting IP flows to the optical-level and as well creating/releasing lambda-connections for them. Network managers would only be required to configure the optical switches in order to instruct them on which flows to look for and when lambda-connections have to be established and released by using GMPLS signaling protocols. Once configured, the optical switches cooperatively work by their own. Figure 1 depicts how our proposal for a self-management of lambda-connections in hybrid networks would look like.

In Figure 1 IP and optical domains coordinate with one another in order to detect IP flows and manage lambda-connections. Both domains are assumed as already been configured by network managers. IP routers located at IP domain B are

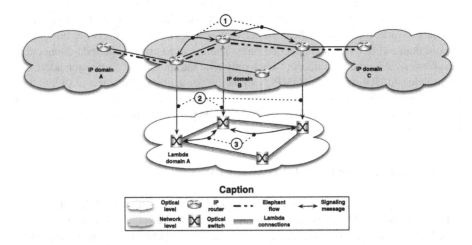

Fig. 1. Self-management of lambda-connection in hybrid networks

exchanging network information (e.g. bandwidth consumed per flow and its duration) regarding to the existence of a elephant flow transiting between IP domains A and C (step 1). Based on this exchanged information and the configuration performed by network managers they make decisions on if a flow is eligible or no longer eligible for a dedicated lambda-connection at the optical-level. If the decision is in favor of creating a lambda-connection (i.e., the elephant flow is eligible to be moved to the optical-level), the IP routers signal the optical switches in lambda domain A (step 2). Then, the optical switches coordinate among themselves in order to create a dedicated lambda-connection to the detected elephant IP flow (step 3). From that point on, the elephant flow is switched at the optical-level and IP routing is accordingly changed. Further information about our self-management approach can be found at [12].

3.2 Functional Architecture

Our functional architecture presents the functional blocks involved in our self-management approach and as well their interaction. Our architecture deals with the layers 1 (Network interface layer) and 2 (Internet layer) of the four-layer TCP/IP network architecture, as can be seen in figure 2.

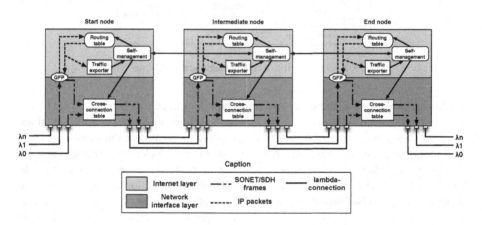

Fig. 2. Self-management functional blocks

Figure 2 shows 4 functional blocks: cross-connection and routing tables, traffic exporter, and a Generic Framing Procedure (GFP) module, which maps IP packets into the underlying transport protocol. In the case of SURFnet6, the underlying transport layer is based on SONET/SDH. Figure 2 also shows our self-management functional block.

The main tasks of the self-management block are to analyze network information and decide when a lambda-connection should be established/released for a certain set of flows. The analysis consists of obtaining network information from the traffic exporter and characterizing it (e.g. by ordering and/or filtering fields). Then, self-management blocks correlate their collected information and cooperatively decide when

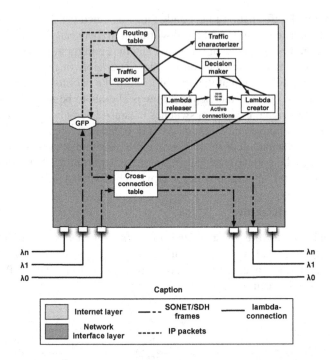

Fig. 3. Zooming in into a self-management functional block

establishing/releasing a lambda-connection. Once decided, the self-management blocks involved in the decision process locally adjust the routing and cross-connection tables. Figure 3 shows more internal details of the self-management functional block.

The self-management functional block is composed by 5 elements: traffic characterizer, decision maker, lambda creator, lambda releaser, and active connections table. The traffic characterizer is in charge of collecting network information exported by the traffic exporter (e.g., a NetFlow exporter) and characterizing it. The characterized information is then sent to the decision maker, which cooperatively decides with other decision makers on moving IP flows from the IP-level to the optical-level and vice-versa.

If a decision to move IP flows to the optical-level is taken, then each decision maker contacts its local lambda creator, which is responsible for establishing lambda-connections. The lambda creator performs that by adjusting the routing and cross-connection tables. Once the lambda-connection is established, the lambda creator adds the new entry in the active connections table. The active connections table lists the current active connections locally held by certain network node.

On the other hand, if a decision to move IP flows back to the IP-level is taken, each decision maker contacts its lambda releaser, which is responsible for tearing down lambda-connections. The lambda releaser then reconfigures the routing and cross-connection tables in order to release the connection. Once the lambda-connection is released, the lambda releaser removes the entry in the active connections table.

3.3   Physical Architecture

The physical architecture consists of showing the physical location of the functional blocks. In our physical architecture, the functional blocks are located at two different physical locations: in the multi-service optical switches and in an external management device. The traffic exporter and routing and cross-connection tables are already supported inside current multi-service optical switches, so they will be kept where they are. This assertion is based on discussions with network managers. The remaining blocks are located in the external management device. Figure 4 shows our physical architecture.

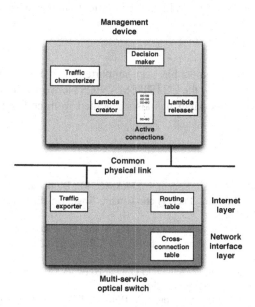

Fig. 4. Physical architecture

Even though all functional blocks could internally be implemented into the multiservice optical switches, doing that is not trivial because vendors may not be willing to change the implementation of the optical switches operating systems. That is the reason our new functional blocks will be implemented in an external management device.

4   Conclusions

Section 2 of this paper identified the current approaches to manage lambda-connection in hybrid networks. In practice two approaches are being used: conventional management, which is based on SNMP or TL1 manager-agent interactions, and GMPLS. Both approaches, however, require human interaction to detect flows and create / release lambda-connections. As discussed in Section 3.1, traditional approaches for lambda-connection management are therefore slow and error prone. To overcome these problems, the remainder of this paper proposed a functional and physical architecture for self-management of lambda-connections.

The functional architecture defines which functions and interactions are needed to perform self-management in a logical and comprehensible way. The physical architecture defines how these functions and interactions can be implemented; an important goal hereby is to avoid as much as possible modifications to current implementations of multi-service optical switches. This decision allows us to create, in later stages of our research, a testbed to evaluate our architecture.

This paper describes work that is still in progress. More research is needed, for instance, to determine proper configuration parameter values for the self-management functional blocks in order to decide when to establish and release a lambda-connection. A next goal is therefore to simulate our architecture in order to find answers for this question.

Acknowledgments

The research on self-management has been supported by SURFnet in the context of the GigaPort-RoN project, and by the EC IST-EMANICS Network of Excellence (#26854). The work presented in this paper has also benefited from collaboration with INRIA Lorraine.

References

1. Gauger, C.M., Kuhn, P.J., Breusegem, E., Pickavet, M., Demeester, P.: Hybrid Optical Network Architectures: Bringing Packets and Circuits Together. IEEE Communications Magazine 44(8), 36–42 (2006)
2. SURFnet: SURFnet6 lighpaths mark start of the new Internet area (press release), Available in: http://www.surfnet.nl/info/en/artikel_content.jsp?objectnumber=107197
3. Bernstein, G., Rajagopalan, B., Saha, D.: Optical Network Control: Architecture, Protocols, and Standards. Addison-Wesley, Reading (2003)
4. Schoenwaelder, J., Quittek, J., Kappler, C.: Building Distributed Management Applications with the IETF Script MIB. IEEE Journal on Selected Areas in Communications 18, 702–714 (2000)
5. Claise, B.: Cisco Systems NetFlow Services Export Version 9. Request for Comments: 3954 (RFC 3954) (2004)
6. Schoenwaelder, J.: Overview of the 2002 IAB Network Management Workshop. Request for Comments: 3535 (RFC 3535) (2003)
7. Case, J., Mundy, R., Partain, D., Stewart, B.: Introduction and Applicability Statements for Internet Standard Management Framework. Request for Comments: 3410 (RFC 3410) (2002)
8. Man, F.-T.: A Brief History of TL1 Journal of Network and Systems Management 7 (1999)
9. Mannie, E.: Generalized Multi-Protocol Label Switching (GMPLS) Architecture. Request for Comments: 3945 (RFC 3945) (2004)
10. Rosen, E.C., Viswanathan, A., Callon, R.: Multi-Protocol Label Switching (GMPLS) Architecture. Request for Comments: 3031 (RFC 3031) (2001)
11. Banerjee, A., Drake, J., Lang, J., Turner, B., Kompella, K., Rekhter, Y.: Generalized Multiprotocol Label Switching: An Overview of Routing and Management Enhancements. IEEE Communications Magazine 39(1), 144–151 (2001)
12. Fioreze, T., Pras, A.: Using self-management for establishing light paths in optical networks: an overview. In: Poster session proceedings of the 12th EUNICE Open European Summer School 2006 (EUNICE 2006), pp. 17–20 (2006)

Author Index

Lecture Notes in Computer Science

For information about Vols. 1–4513

please contact your bookseller or Springer